RETURNING

KIRLI SAUNDERS

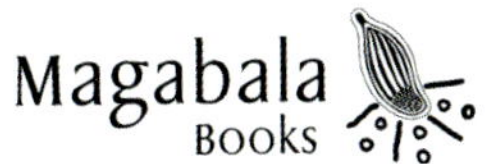

This is a Magabala Book

LEADING PUBLISHER OF ABORIGINAL AND TORRES STRAIT ISLANDER STORYTELLERS.

CHANGING THE WORLD, ONE STORY AT A TIME.

First published 2023
Magabala Books Aboriginal Corporation
1 Bagot Street, Broome, Western Australia
Website: www.magabala.com
Email: sales@magabala.com

Magabala Books receives financial assistance from the Commonwealth Government through the Australia Council, its arts advisory body. The State of Western Australia has made an investment in this project through the Department of Local Government, Sport and Cultural Industries. Magabala Books would like to acknowledge the support of the Shire of Broome, Western Australia.

Magabala Books is Australia's only independent Aboriginal and Torres Strait Islander publishing house. Magabala Books acknowledges the Traditional Owners of the Country on which we live and work. We recognise the unbroken connection to traditional lands, waters and cultures. Through what we publish, we honour all our Elders, peoples and stories, past, present and future.

Cover and internal design by Jo Hunt
Original typeset and design by Post Pre-press Group
Printed in China by Everbest Printing Company

ISBN (Print) 978-1-922613-70-7
ISBN (ePDF) 978-1-922613-69-1

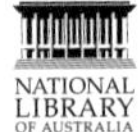

A catalogue record for this book is available from the National Library of Australia

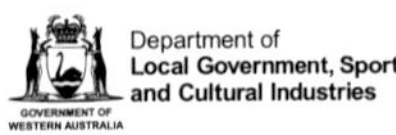

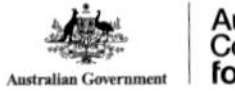

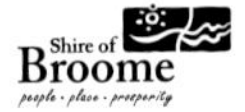

I pay my respects to the Elders past and present of these lands, seas and skies, and to all Custodians caring for Country across this continent. I give thanks to my Ancestors, Family and Community who shape my path, and who have supported me on this journey. *Returning* was written across many lands, predominantly Dharawal, Yuin and Gundungurra, where I was raised or now reside and where I have kinship ties.

CONTENTS

RAGE + GRACE

HEALING

FOREWORD

While creating *Returning* our communities encountered fires, floods and the pandemic.

We consumed the news, left food out for wallabies in scorched landscapes, sent care packs to strangers, danced for rain and willed it to stop. We mourned our homes, our sacred places and our non-human relatives. We confronted the harsh reality of eco-grief, climate crisis and the desperate need to care for Mother Earth.

And all from isolation as COVID kept us inside, on Zoom, with our caffeine addictions and dogs.

Amid the pandemic, we protested from socially distanced safety as the Black Lives Matter movement received a hashtag. We saw the issues that our Ancestors and we have been fighting become mainstream (for a time). We witnessed a swell of solidarity as awareness of deaths in custody, and numbers of lives lost, continued/s to rise. We tried to raise the age, and to protect our waterways, land and skies with cultural burn and petition after petition.

We're still fighting.

In the pandemic, we lost loved ones or they were kept safely distanced from us. We found anxiety in isolation. We read, listened to podcasts, made sourdough and art. We planted gardens to keep the time. We found our dark parts and inside those, we found clarity. Which made us get married and have babies, or leave our jobs and partners.

In the first lockdowns on Dharawal and Yuin lands, I did the latter two, finally embracing a big dream of full-time freelancing and my queerness.

I sat more comfortably in my loud, matriarchal, joyful self, with easing heteronormative and patriarchal beliefs I'd subscribed to. I also danced with a neurodivergent diagnosis and witnessed my own mental health in a new light.

I completed yoga teaching training to counter my perceived limitations and learnt to ask for help from kin and medical professionals. I moved, meditated and journalled. I rode shotgun when I couldn't drive, swapped my motorbike for a 'lectric pushy, sang around campfires and surfed (under supervision).

I cried.

I swam in the ocean. I made art.

I found more feathers than I did when life was fast.

And in the honey moments, slow and sticky, I travelled home, to Mum's Country, Yuin Land, and Gran's Country, Gunai Land. I played footy with Pop's team, La Pa, and spent more time connecting with our Dharawal ties. And on the land that birthed my family, I sat under trees, by the river and sea, and nestled in the knowing of my Old People.

I spent three months outside of my locked-down state, learning from other clans in the Northern Territory and Western Australia. I walked songlines, caught dinner, shared stories, rode horses through the Kimberley, picked bush raisins with Elders. I learnt new language words. I taught young ones to write poems about climate change and together we planted seeds with hope.

And <u>all of this</u> has been my undoing.

This body of art and poetry is a work of *Returning* to a truer self. It is a snapshot of moments on a path that is still (will always be) unfolding.

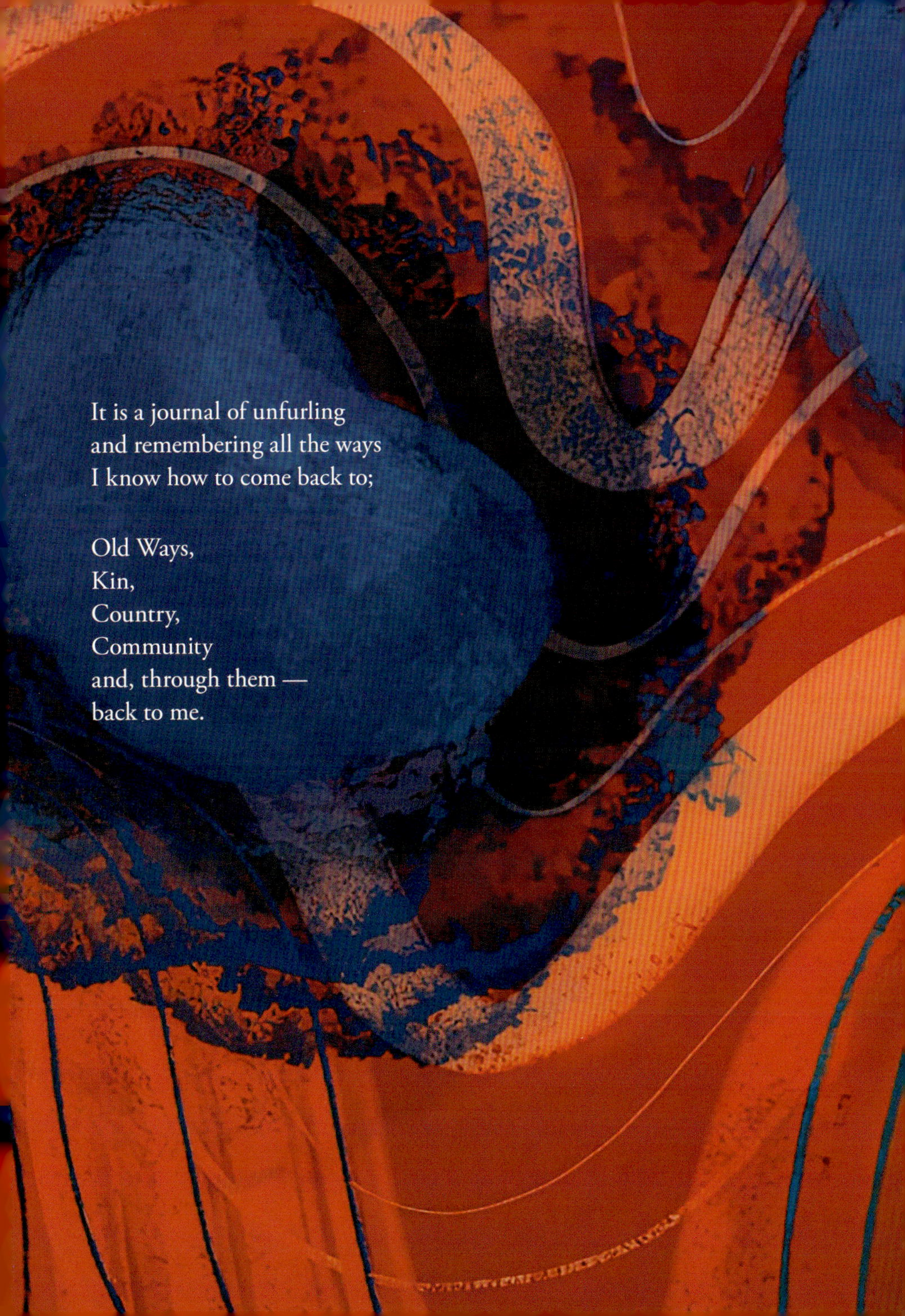

It is a journal of unfurling
and remembering all the ways
I know how to come back to;

Old Ways,
Kin,
Country,
Community
and, through them —
back to me.

ACKNOWLEDGMENT OF COUNTRY

Today I honour the Traditional Owners
of these lands
shaped by sacred creation spirits
and pay my respect to their
deep knowing —
passed down
through cell and story

I honour their culture
and care for Country —
Water and Skies

I honour their survival
for millennia
despite it all

I acknowledge my role in
truth telling
in caring
for Mother Earth

for alpine mauve burr-daisy
sawfish in salted estuary
for bell birds, curlew and gouldian finch
corroboree frog
antarctic beech trees
pygmy possum
atlas moth
spotted quoll
glossy black cockatoo
blue whale
and coral

I acknowledge my role in protecting her remaining wild places
the forest | river | reef
desert | scrub
marshland | mountain |
great blue
above

with the same loving kindness the Old People have always shown her

and like the wise ones,
I promise
to move everywhere
with care

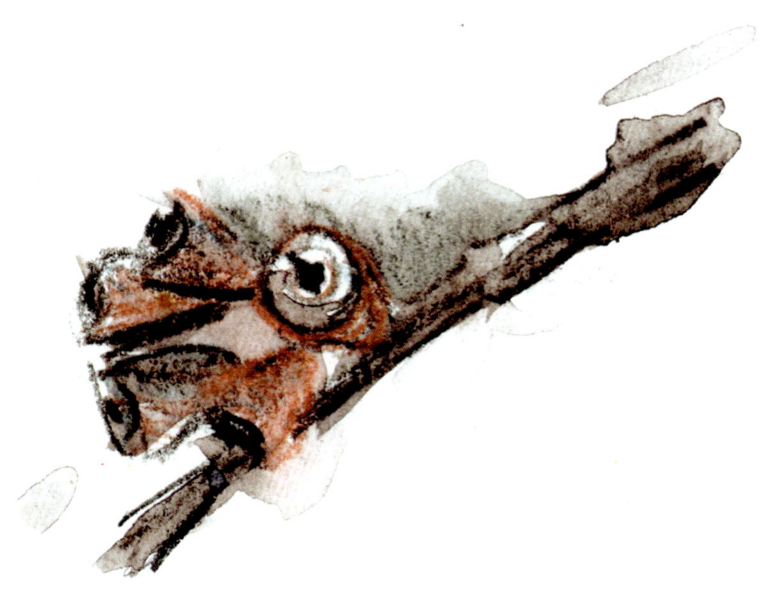

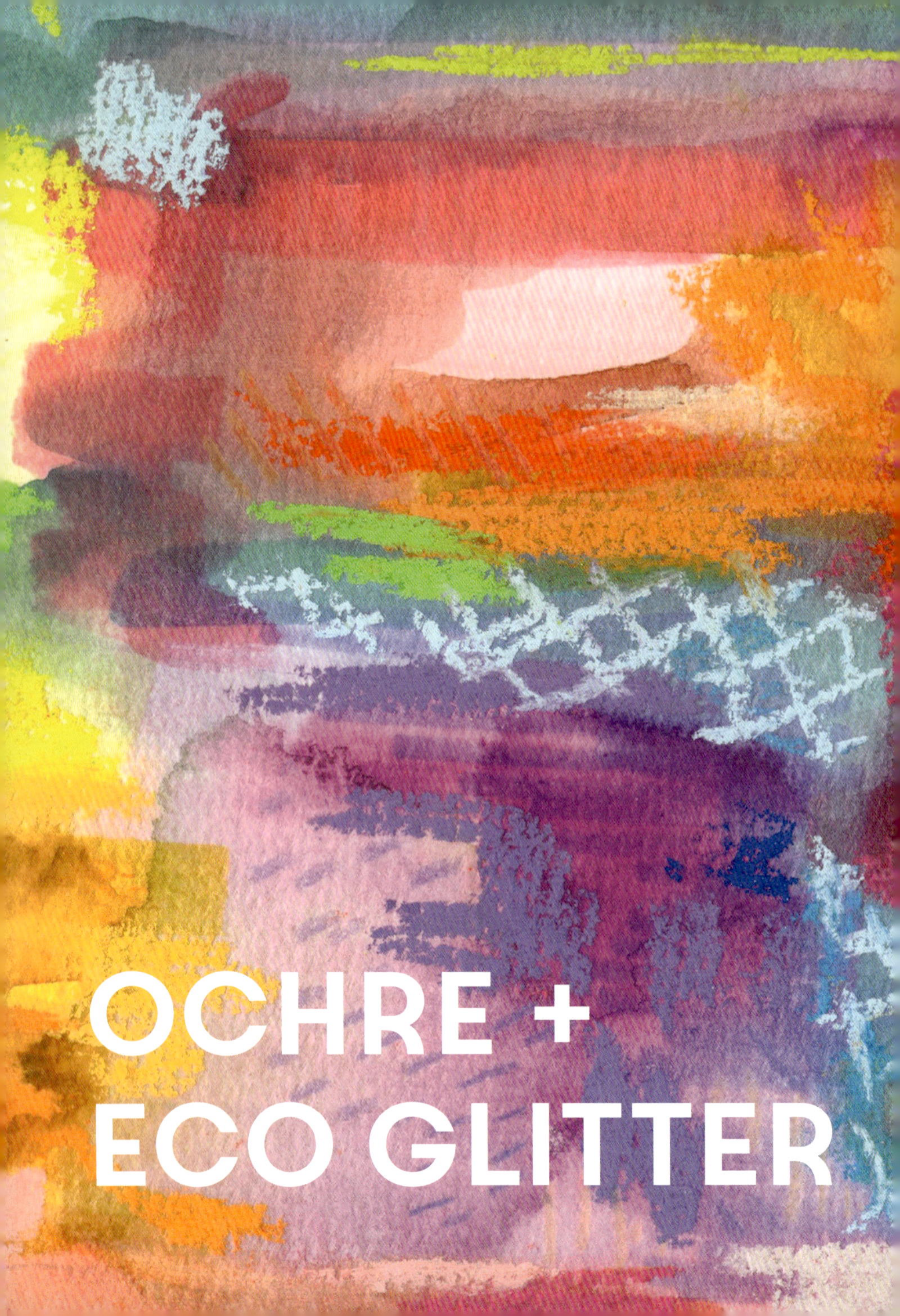
OCHRE +
ECO GLITTER

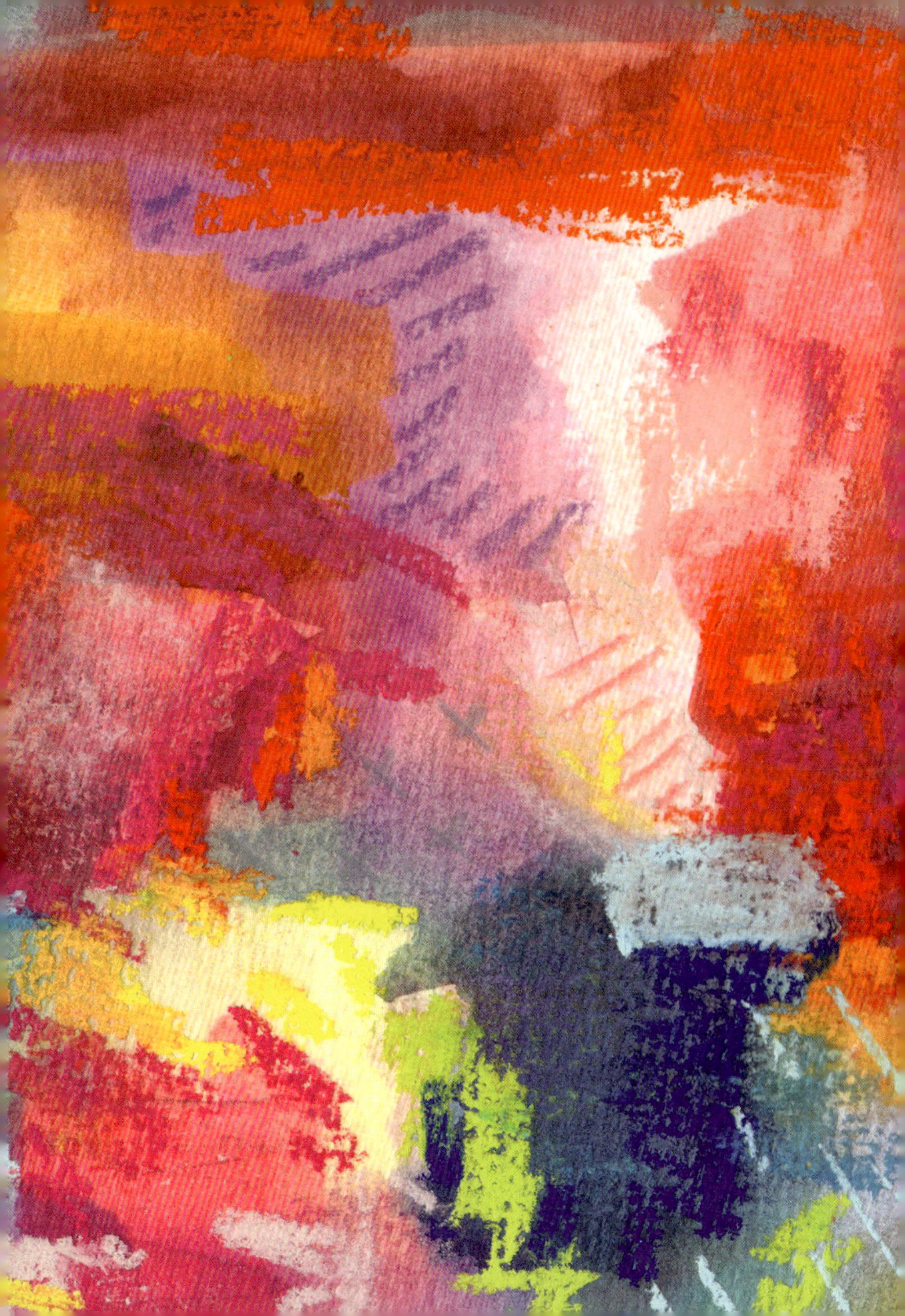

~~title~~ | Tidal

Oscillating between channels —
we watch them
victim-blame La Niña
and her trade winds
which surge east
drawing cool water
from the D
E
E
P
to surface
Earth's heat.

On screen,
pollies are indiscreet with euphemism, casting
Climate Change as *hot flush,*
Assault as *allegation.*

We change the station
understanding denial and
gendered violence are
everywhere —

here, they gaslight the sky —
silence the cries and rain
that flow heavy
over our Mother
while another mum
wades waters
to rescue
her own.

soon the torrent will subside

but nothing could hide the line of a tide
from the moontime memory
of a Woman

On the news
they justify worth with relation,
mistaking
that for protection
a female needs
a title.

Ngurra responds with ~T~I~D~A~L~
o v e r f l o w of her own
she takes up [space],
evacuates hθmes,
raises dam walls,
and closes the coast.

Ngurra shows that she could <u>never</u> be too much
encouraging trust in the s\w\e\l\l of rage
that arrives in us
as charges pressed,
our en-masse march,
allies by survivors,
and 100-year flood.

Ngurra – meaning home, camp and Country in many First Nations languages and dialects across the continent.

When *Ngurra* says ***enough is enough***
the world stops to listen

and like her, our vision
for justice
will not
go unheard —

they cannot disregard
the waves of change
we make

when we rise like
Water
Mother
Women
One.

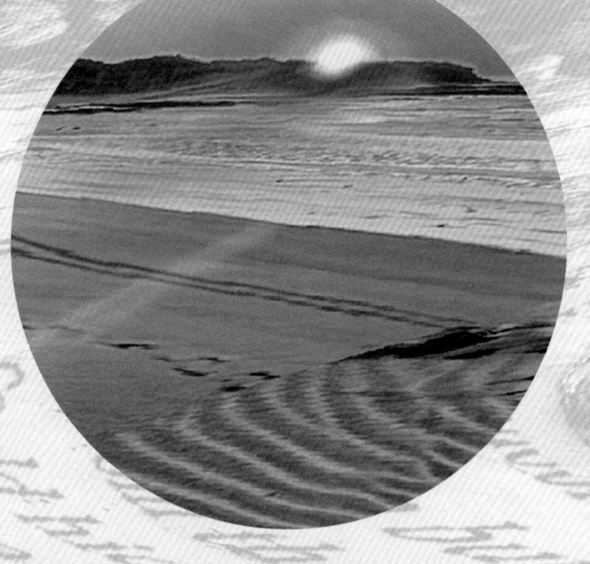

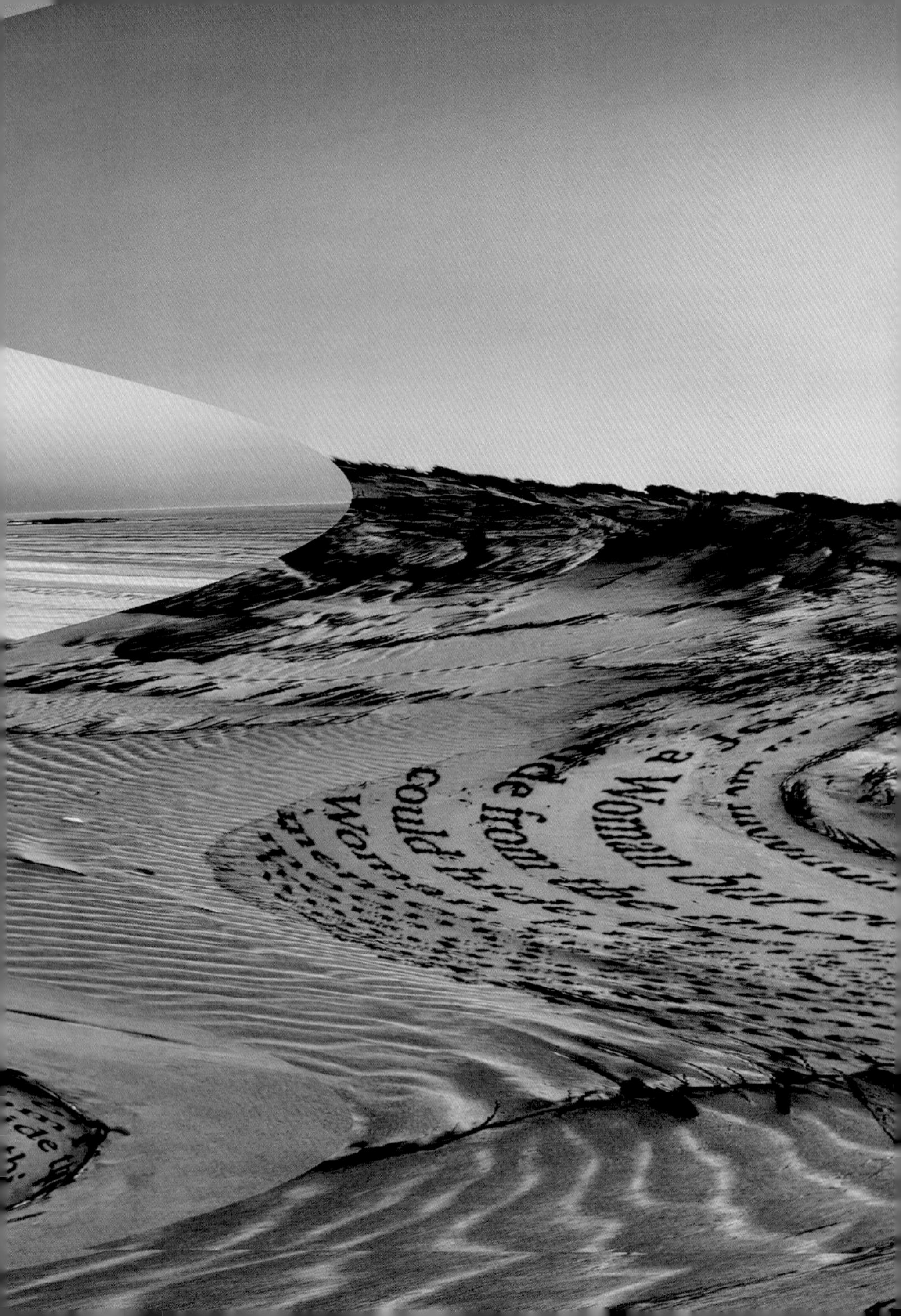
a Woman
de from the
Could
Word

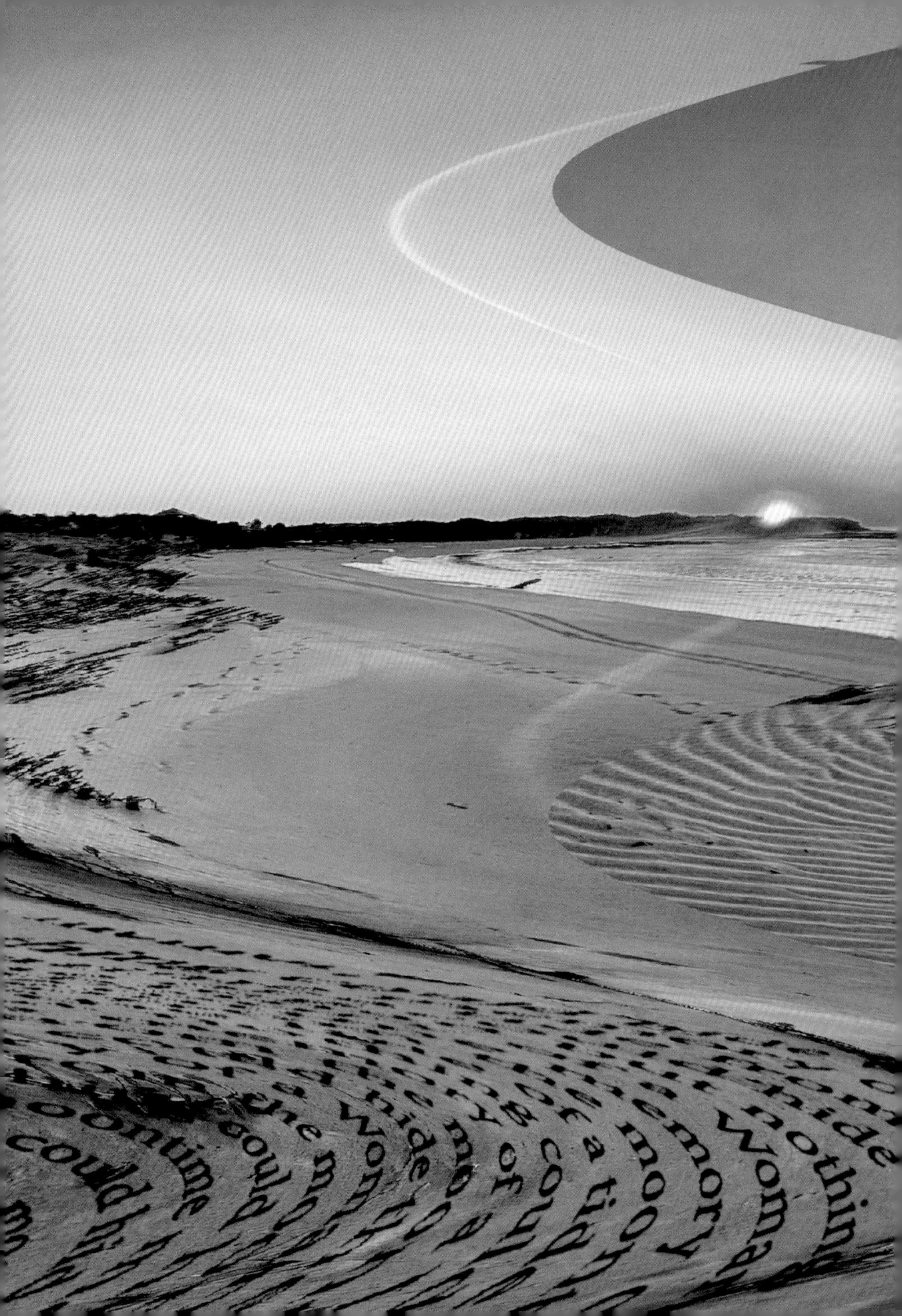

Brave

Thank you
the Black and Brown bodies that
s
t
o
o
d for Liberation
who rioted
before supremacy dirtied that word

thank you spirits who b|a|r|r|i|c|a|d|e|d streets
in the face of police
so parades of rainbows
and survival
could ensue

each year
we are still here
all eco glitter and ochre
honouring **you**

thank you Loved Ones
who wove c\o\r\n\r\o\w\s as maps
\with seeds\
\ [inside] \

danced when the ground was hard

sang in language
and rebellion

told Dreaming stories
under the table for little lungs to carry forth
thank you Grandmother Trees
still standing

resolute

thank you Aunties
in Parliament
here and Overseas

thank you Sisters honouring
your God
and dismantling
patriarchy
in spaces of
worship

thank you every
Yes vote
in referendum
and plebiscite

thank you privilege
and ableism checkers

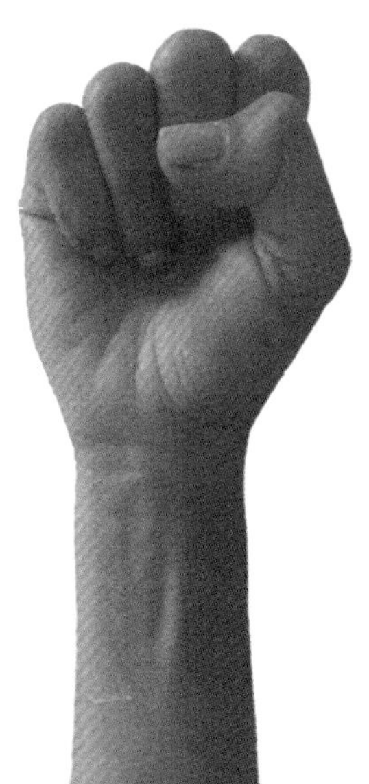

thank you education equality
accessibility,
and climate change activists

thank you lawyers
and magistrates
for prosecuting perpetrators
of hate —

our bodies have always been our own

thank you LGBTQIA+ fam
for being unapologetically
you

I hope soon
Brave
won't be the label we choose
for humans pursuing freedom and truth

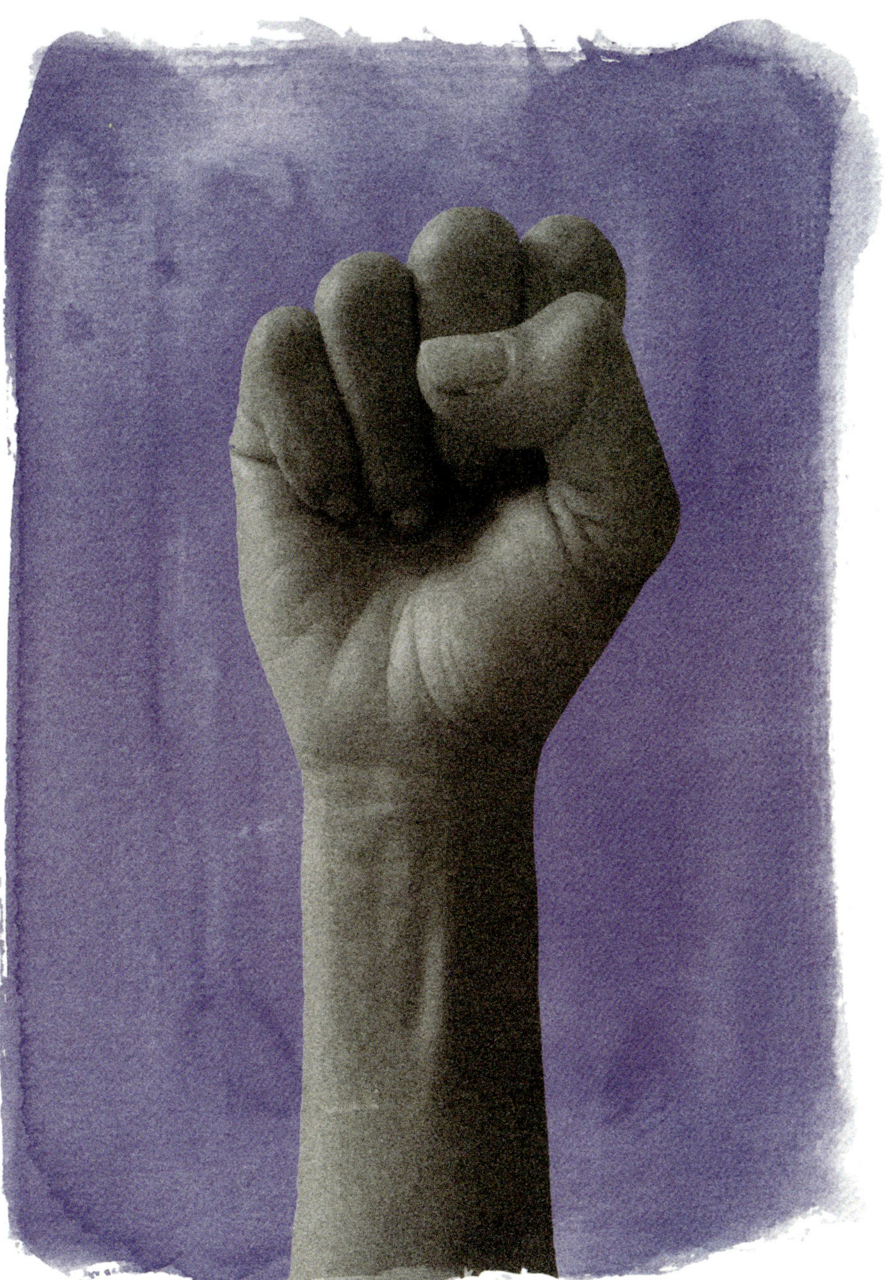

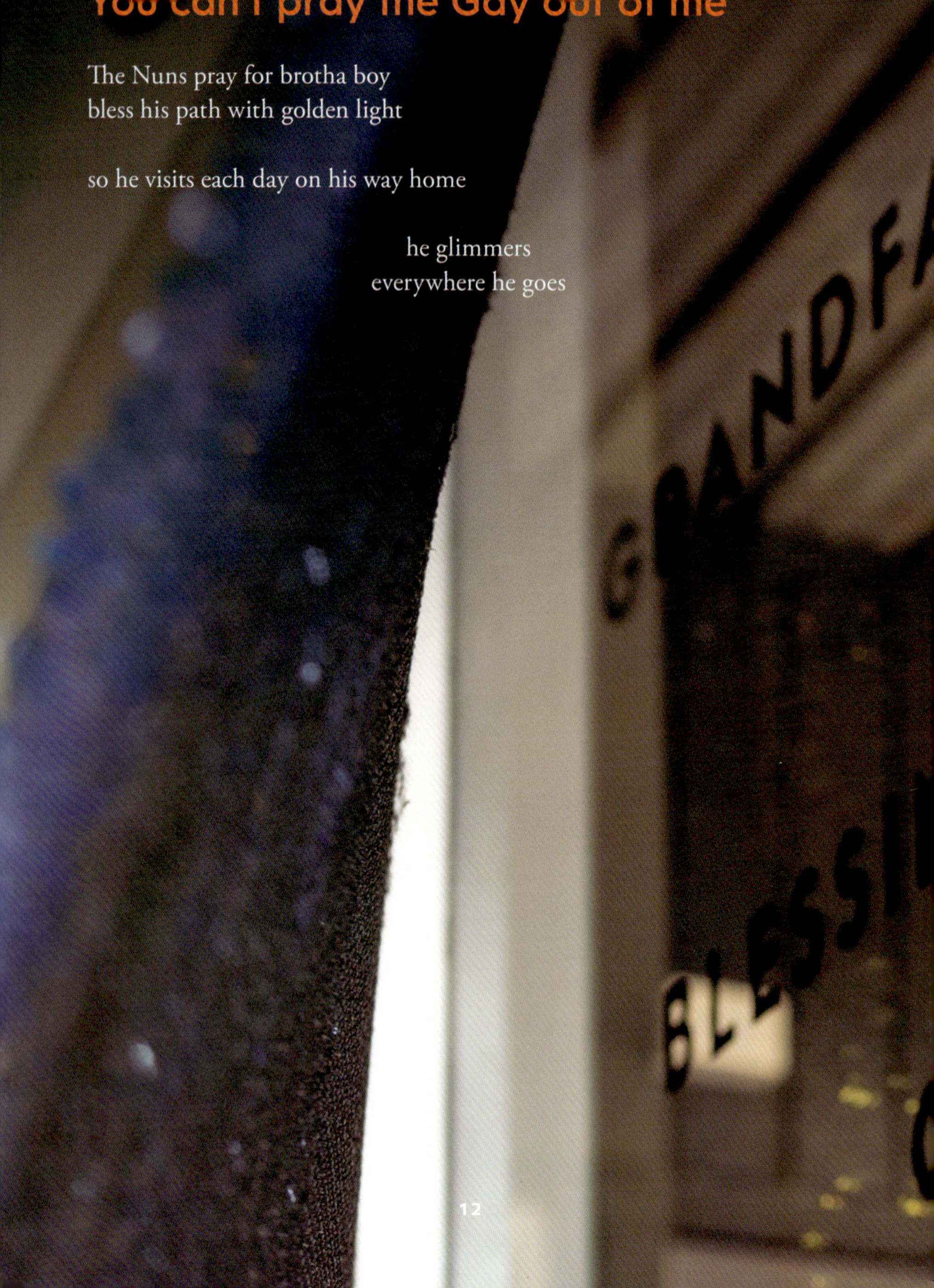

You can't pray the Gay out of me

The Nuns pray for brotha boy
bless his path with golden light

so he visits each day on his way home

he glimmers
everywhere he goes

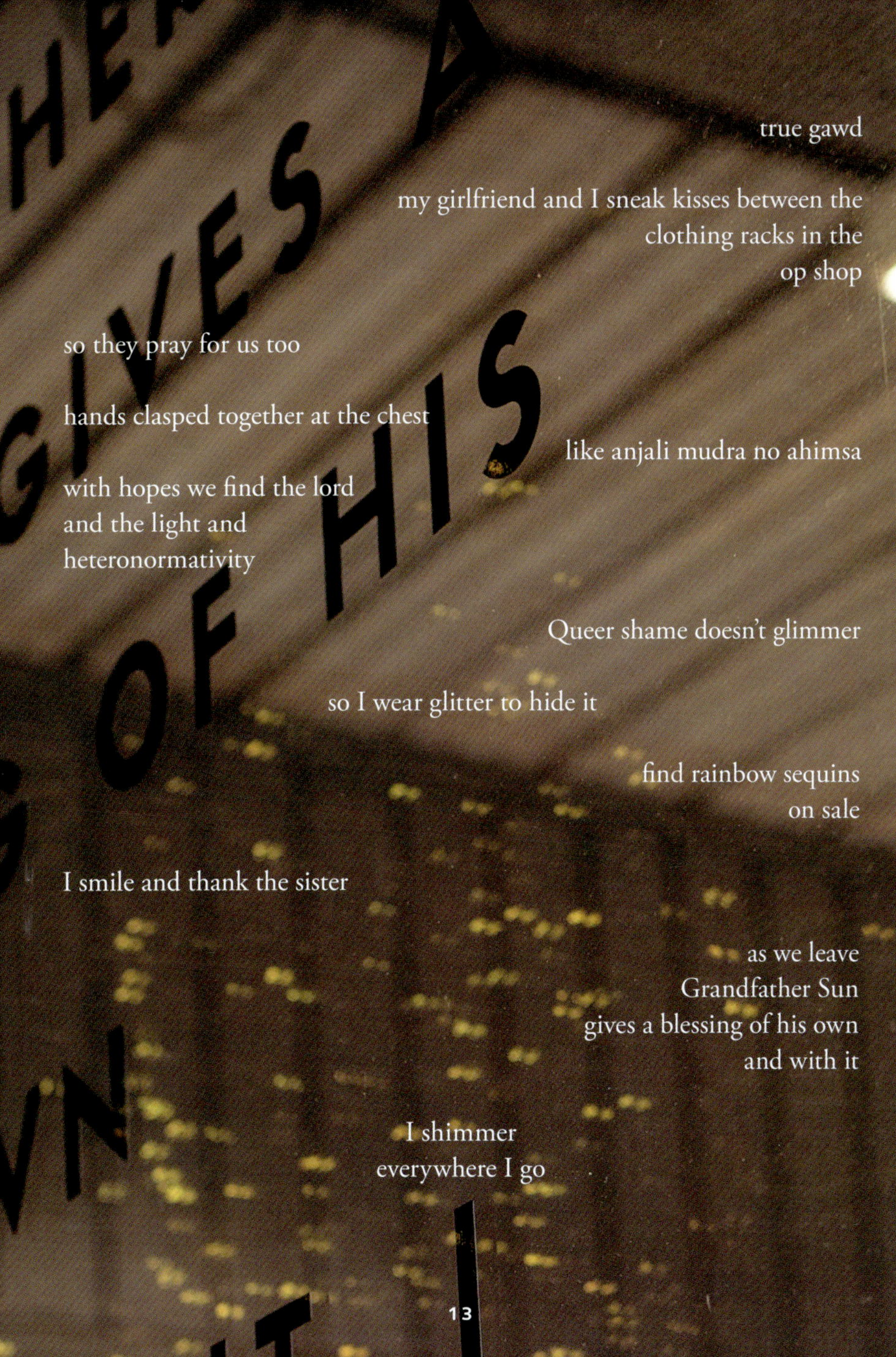

true gawd

my girlfriend and I sneak kisses between the
clothing racks in the
op shop

so they pray for us too

hands clasped together at the chest

like anjali mudra no ahimsa

with hopes we find the lord
and the light and
heteronormativity

Queer shame doesn't glimmer

so I wear glitter to hide it

find rainbow sequins
on sale

I smile and thank the sister

as we leave
Grandfather Sun
gives a blessing of his own
and with it

I shimmer
everywhere I go

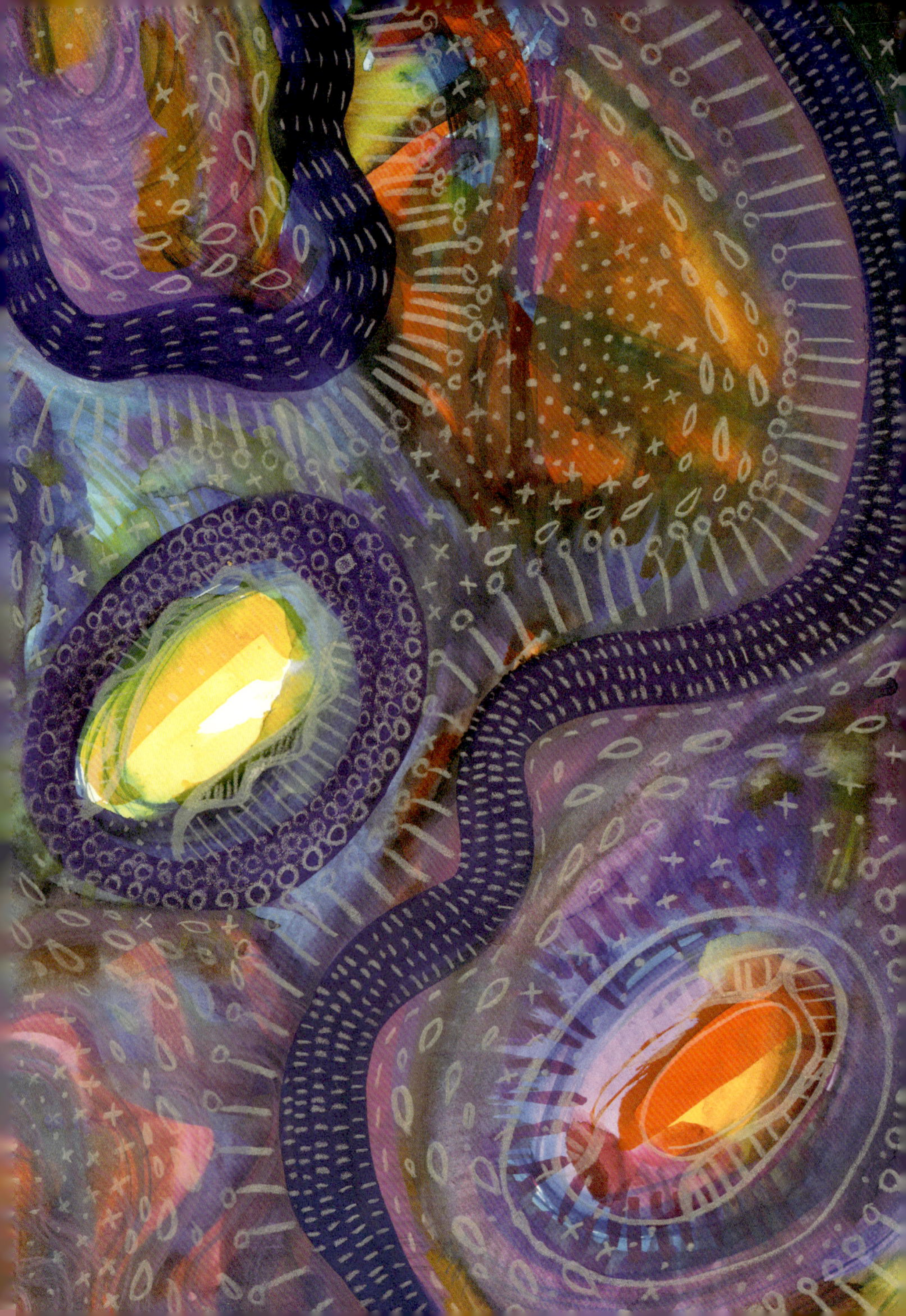

We are Marching Because

~ for International Women's Day

We are marching because
Parliament doesn't employ enough
of our sisters as ministers,
and sinister lovers
take a wife a week
to the grave.

We are marching
to save
girls being married
too young
and unwilfully,

and because
the probability
that we'll be
sexually assaulted
is one in three.

We are marching because
though we have degrees
in business and medicine
men are employed
in our place.

We are marching
to erase
a salary gap
that has women paid

at the same rate
as men
a decade
ago,

marching to show
solidarity with
women locked up
for not paying fines,
to feed their babies

marching against
swines that
commit genital mutilation
and for the advocation
that this cease.

We are marching
for mothers —
who still face
regular workplace discrimination.

We are marching
for every
'me too',

me too

marching for the option
to choose,

and for every time
we have felt less
than Goddess.

We are here to bless
the divine feminine
within,

to tout the success
of the women
who raised us,
and to echo their tenacious feet
on the streets of this town
in resounding agreeance
that we won't back down

until we're equal.

A catalogue of the times I've come out so far:

to my boyfriend at the time
to family, who
    said 'you do you my girl, love is love'
    doubted and asked if I was sure
    told me 'should have gone to church more … bloody gays are
    ruining the sanctity of marriage … you know two mums raising
    kids ain't right …'
to friends that
    acted surprised
    threw high fives at me and asked if 'we're having a coming out party?'
    grew rage red under collar and quizzed if 'I'm dating *her* or what?'
    stated bluntly, 'you know you can still screw women, be straight and
    stay with your boyfriend don't you?'
to Elders that
    encouraged, 'oh great Bub, you bring her a cuppa next time you
    come through'
to my baby cousins
    who giggled and said 'is other aunty going too?'
to a doctor
    who cautioned against coming off contraception until I explained
to the gynecologist (who assumed I was straight)
    and who elaborated on same sex ways of conceiving

to my colleagues and boss
to my hairdresser
to my barista
	who cheered 'yessssss sistaaa! Join. The. Club.'
to my ex
to my chiropractor
to the insurance company
	that asked steely 'and has your girlfriend been driving for more than 10 years?'
to the florist
	'oh! my mate is gay too!!'
to my sports team
to the lady at the massage parlour
	who asked if we are 'sisters or friends?'
to the fella in the surf
and to the ones who slid into my DMs
	despite the rainbow emoji in my bio
and to myself
	over and over again
	over and over again

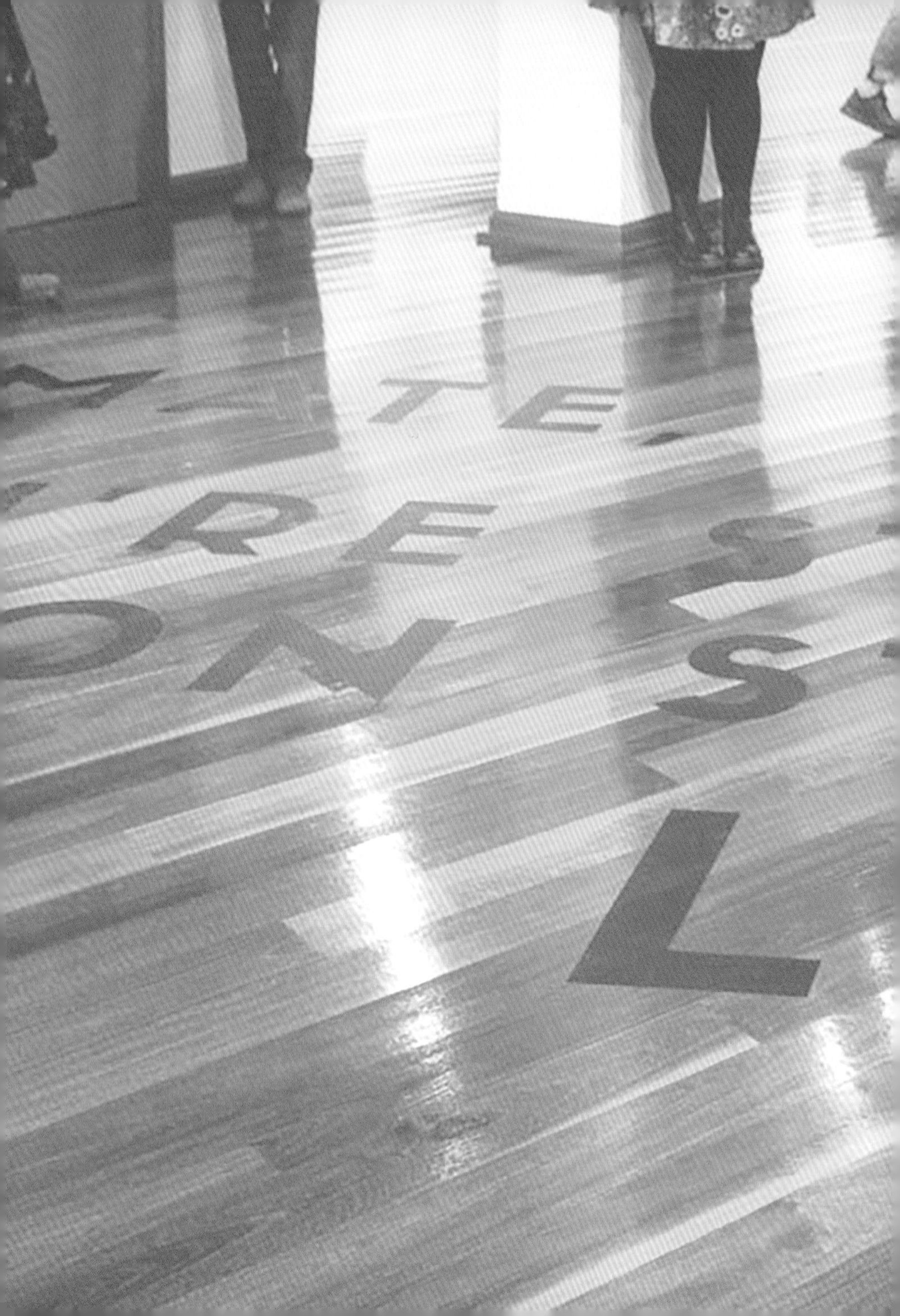

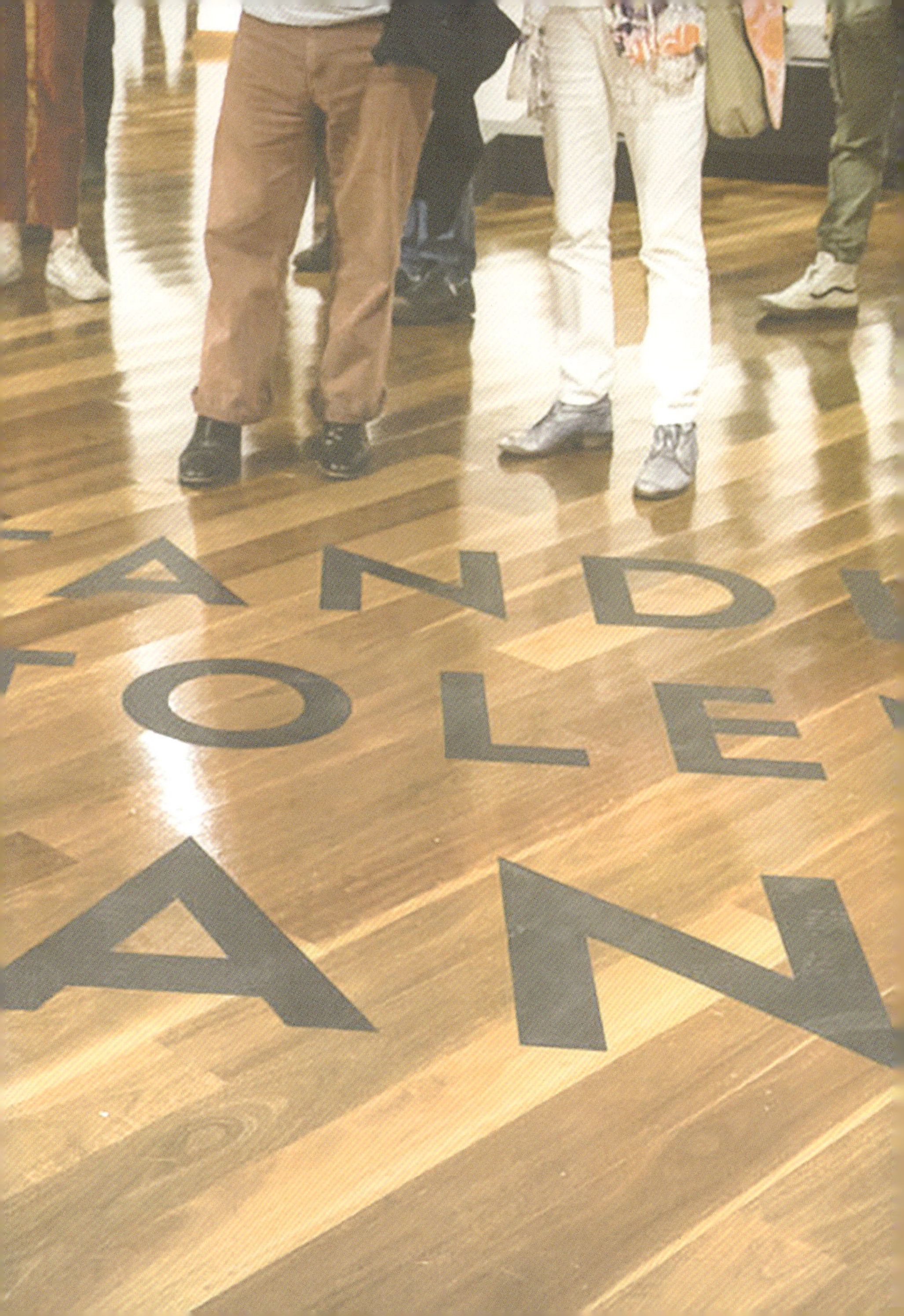
AND
OLE
AN

Mate You're Standing on Stolen Land

~ After Tuck and Ree, who taught us *'Decolonisation is not a metaphor, because at some point, we're going to have to talk about returning stolen land'.*

After class
one of the participants calls

he's just yarned with the local cop shop

said he wanted to understand theft
'it means taking something that isn't yours'

asked if something stolen can be sold for profit
'that's a crime as well, Sir, do you know of something that's been
stolen and then sold?'

clarified that it applies to objects
and land
'yes'

wanted to know if homicide and genocide were also illegal
'yes, that is correct'

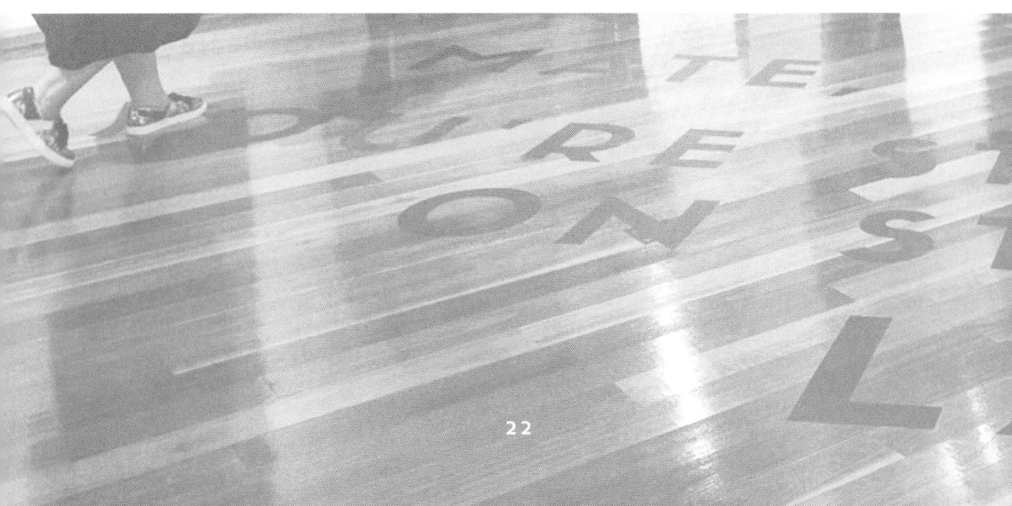

stated clearly then, that he knew about something
'ok, can you tell me more'

said, we all knew about something
'sorry Sir, I'm unsure what you're talking about'

you know, sovereignty was never ceded
...
mate, you're standing on stolen land
...
genocide and many other crimes were/are committed here
...
we profit off it every day in this settler-colonial state
...
Treaty might go some of the way to healing

the cop sighed audibly.

Guess he didn't have much to say.

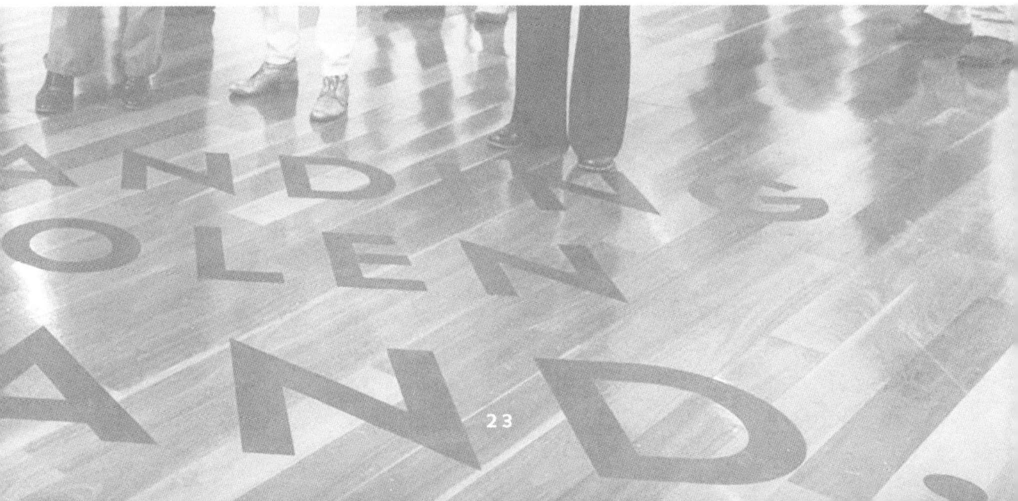

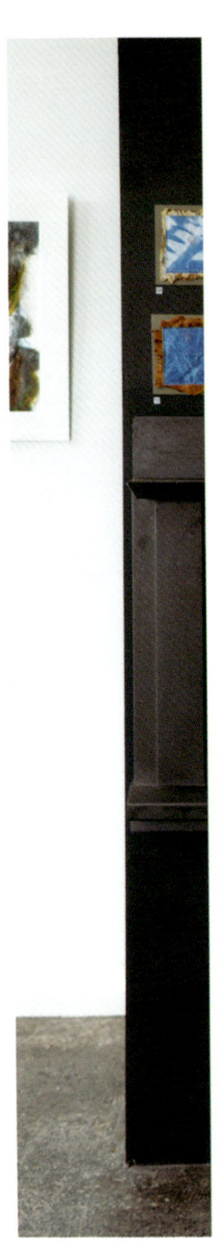

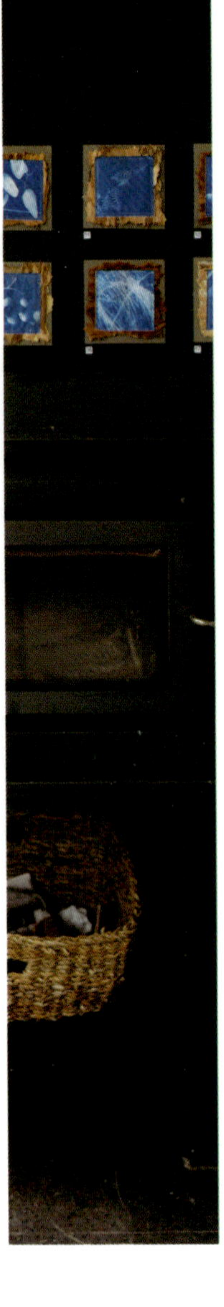
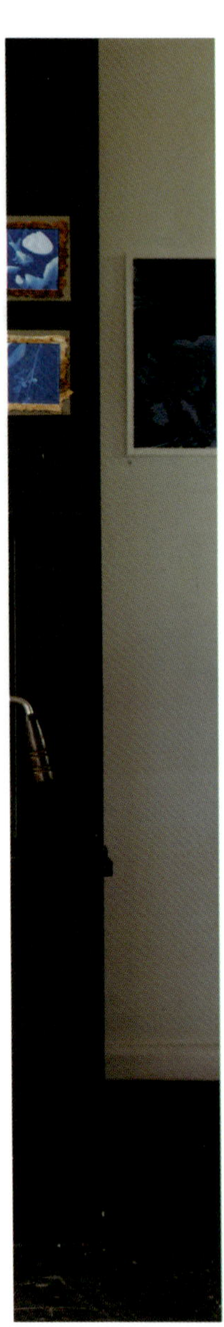

Wallflowers and Evergreens

I count the threads in the rug
on my psychologist's floor

gaze lowered
eye contact avoidant

this is how I find feathers
but don't see the spirits
that leave them

she tells me
rage's underbelly
is *grief*

I imagine thumbing
sacred geometry —
fronds soft in palms
toes s e p a r a t e d
by summered grass
and bark peels

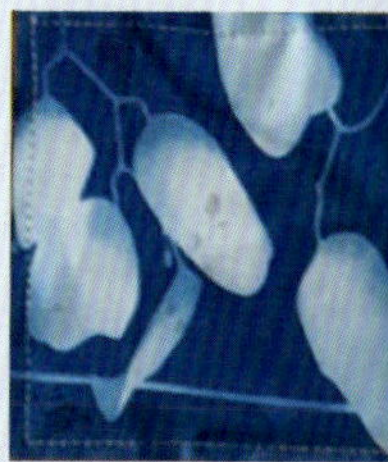

the eucalyptus
staining the air blue
where the hues
of beauty

are seen through tears
and this
elation and depth
are welcomed
simultaneously

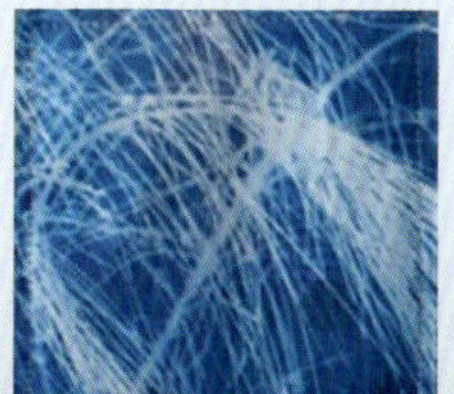

I return to sterility
and wonder
how to be (held)

in spaces
devoid of seasons

where time is measured by
clockface
and replaces
eucalyptus blooming
echidna trains
winds that change
moon who wanes

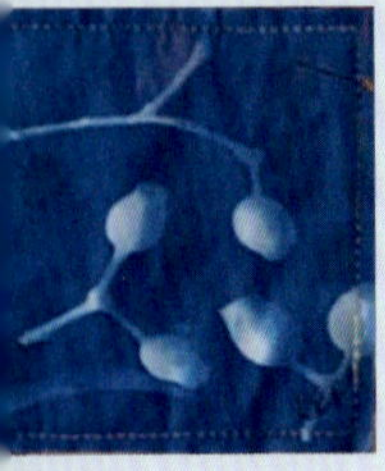

I think rage
must be manufactured
in the same place as
plastic plants

with the willingness to wilt
withdrawn

softness
starched and sewn

fragility
propped up
by falsity

for appearances

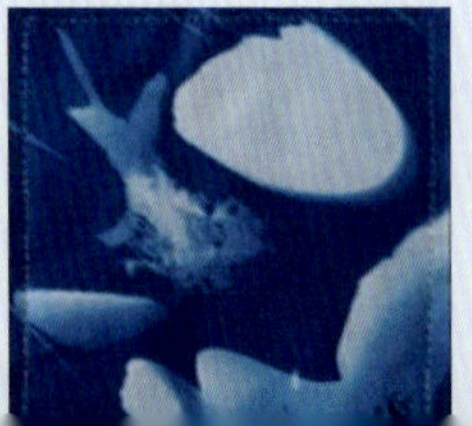

I imagine us
fabricating ourselves
to be
in the world

all wallflowers and evergreens

I realise
I trust more deeply
in the tree
that releases
its seeds
after it
burns

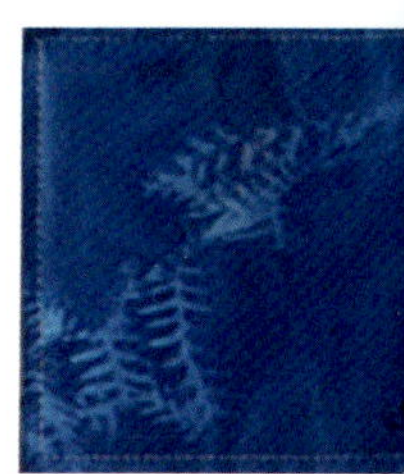

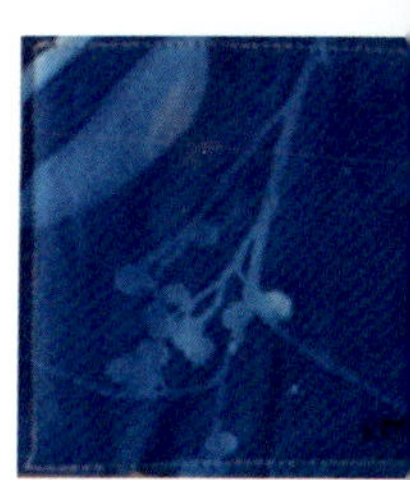

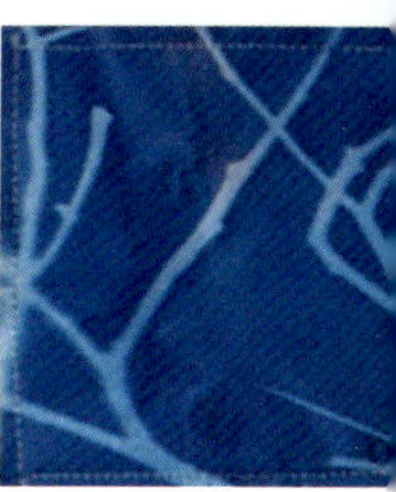

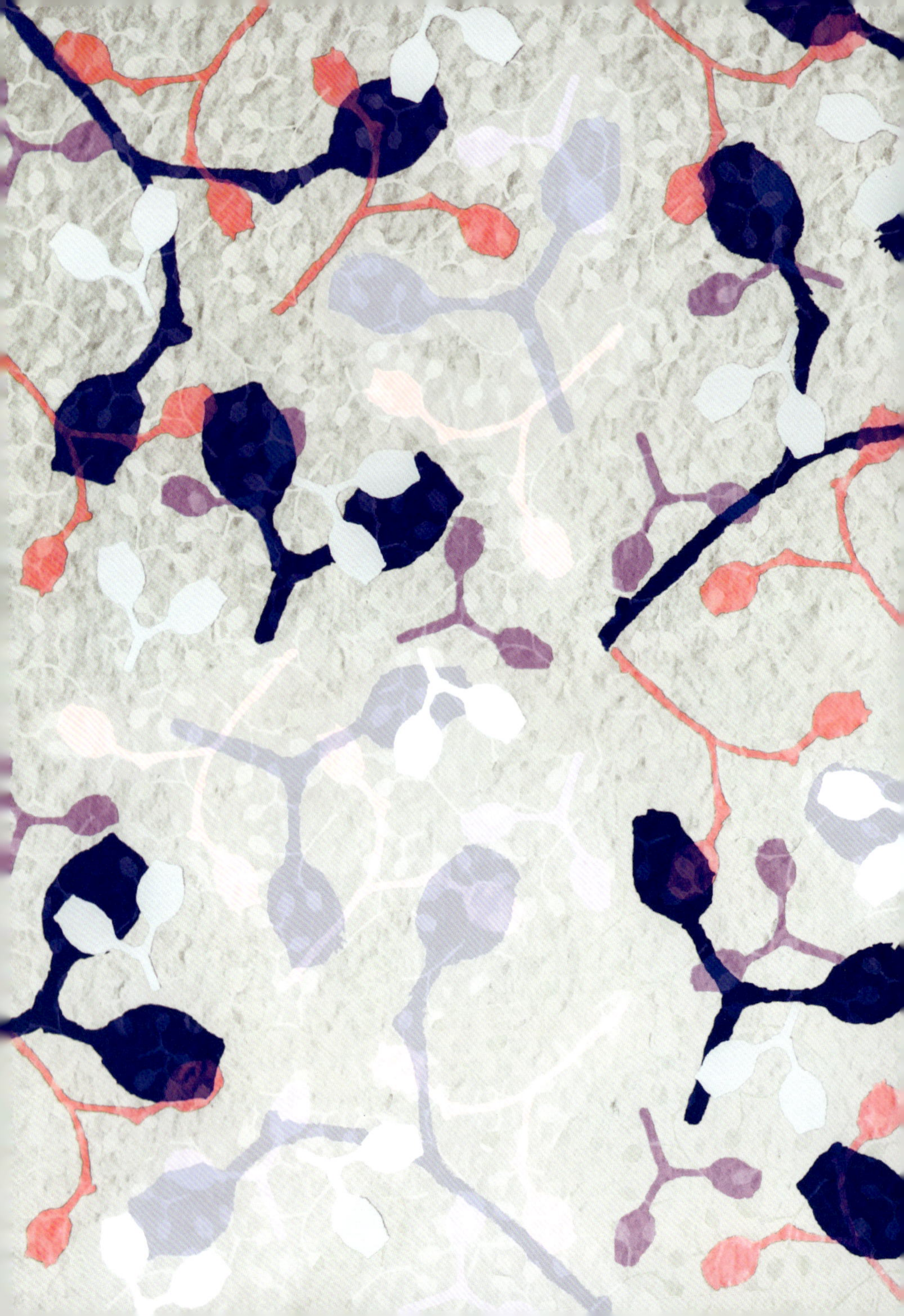

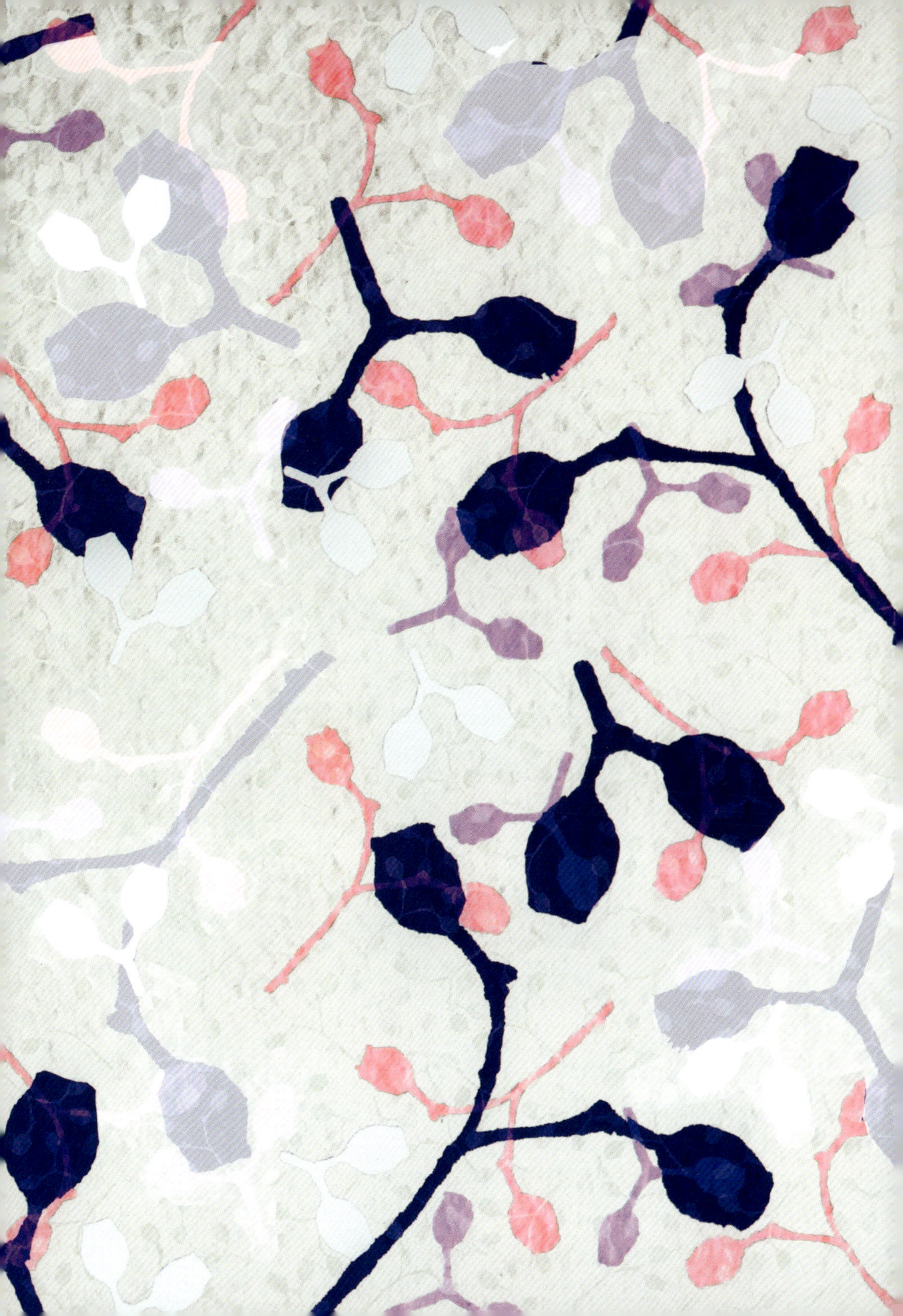

Yadingji

~ After Ross Gay and their *Catalog of Unabashed Gratitude*

Yadingji
weeds with snow globe heads
that dot the unmown path

and yadingji
atlas leaves
broad and medicinal
that lay between

ants who
know the way
through them

yadingji grass —
hard to draw well and
so necessary for our pictures

and seeds
that nestle between blades
to nourish winged things

yadingji feathers that hold the winged ones afloat
for the nakedness beneath
we never see
and rarely think about
but still Love

Yadingji – Dharawal meaning appreciation, or my gratitude. Written and spoken here with sincere Yadingji to my brothers, Ray, Jacob, Joel and Drew.

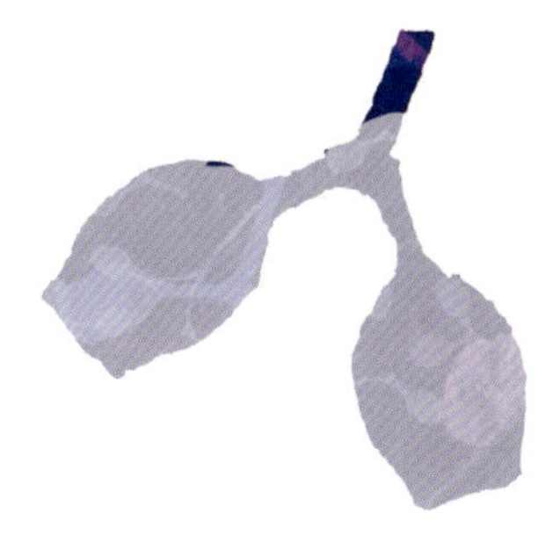

yadingji
glass we watch the clouds through
and the house
shaped around their holdings
thank you homes old
made new again
by family recipes, love and paint

yadingji land,
stolen
and sold under houses
and thank you sovereign warriors
who fight for return
and for all of the souls
who know they cannot be owned

yadingji spirits
who hold the 'tamed ones'
as they uncage themselves

and yadingji
the struggle
and journeys we're all on

yadingji the loved ones
who went away
and the plants they left behind
and thank you
velvet flowers that return
to us each season

yadingji the pre-loved clothes
that weave us into warmth
as summer takes with it mangoes
and autumn arrives with blackberries

yadingji the fruit juice stained lips
that were shaped
in a Grandmother's womb

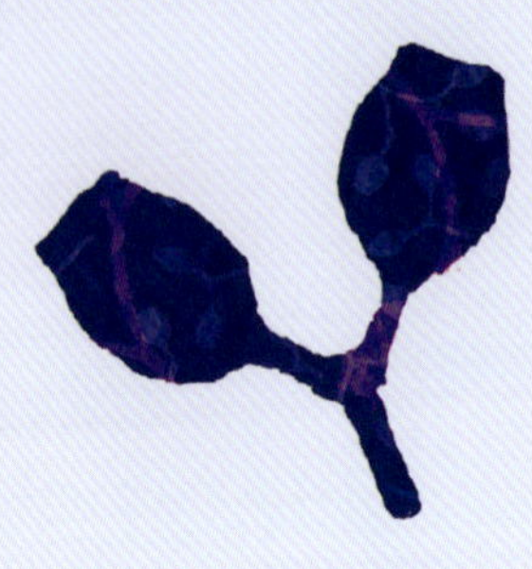

yadingji the Mothers
who carried us
and the Fathers
who taught us love

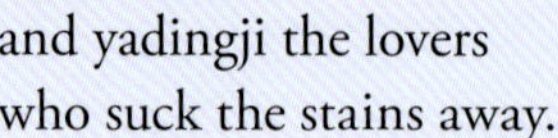

and yadingji the lovers
who suck the stains away.

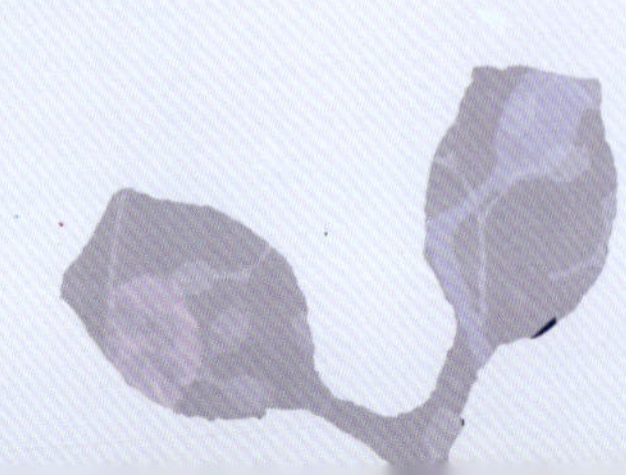

First Kiss

There's a decade of therapy in her kiss —

cognition rewired with queer desires
self validated | long awaited | release in peacemaking with craving
in savoured behaviours
intimate
and right

emboldened by a night in her arms

where alarms of expectation

about *who you are*
and *who you love*
and *how*
are silenced
and the burying of your fullness ends

there's transcendence in allowing what you always knew

in unsubscribing from
skewed world views

and labels
which never describe

who you truly are

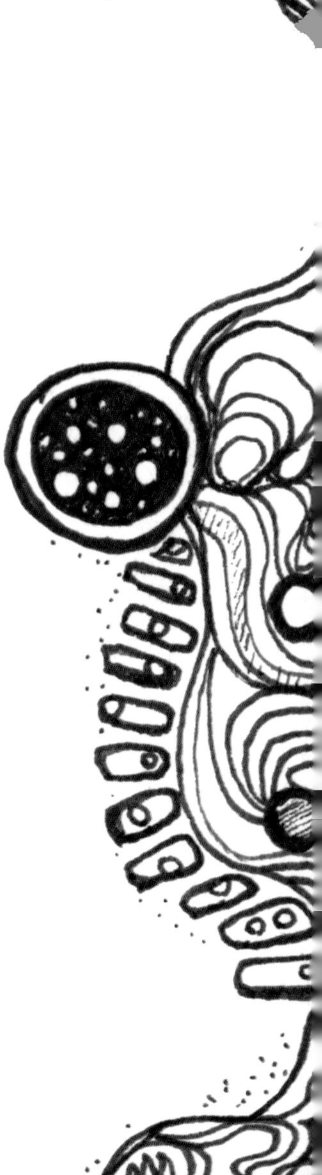

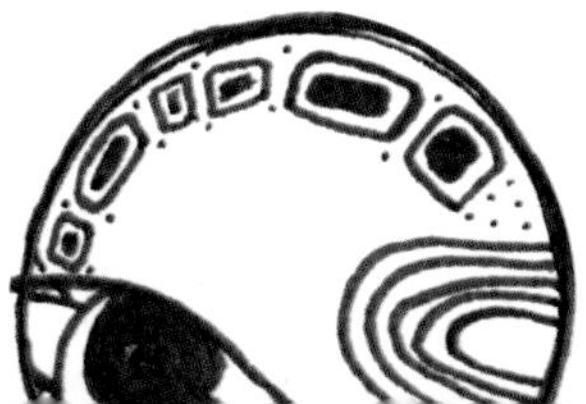

in embracing your heart's
longest longings
and in lingering lips

there's a decade of therapy in her kiss.

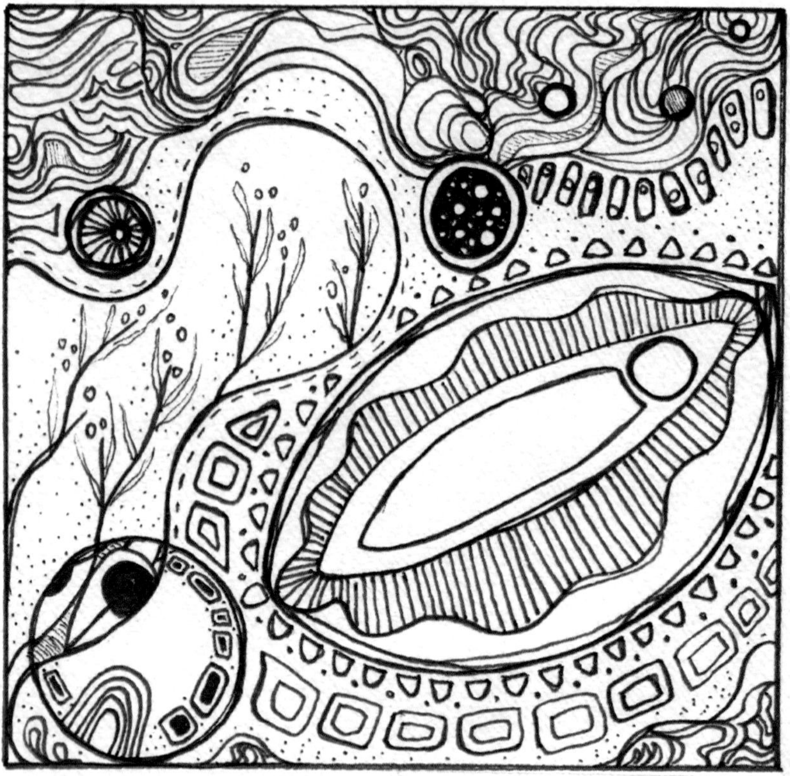

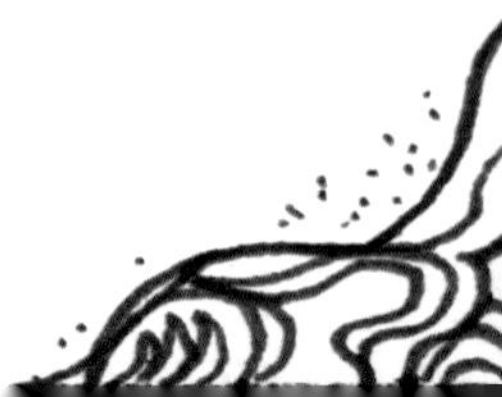

Sacred

Hold me sacred

like the plover's egg
caged in mirrigang's mouth
smooth shell on sharpened teeth
that won't pierce

like sprinkled rain on wild orchid petals
huddled in thunderstorm

like space junk
and meteor dust
s u s p e n d e d

like butterfly's wings
salvaged in curious toddler hands

like the first bite of the season —
pigface
bush cherry
fig

like a long cuppa with Nan

a nest you found

the black cockatoo feather
rosy or golden

like a knowing smile

shark's tooth

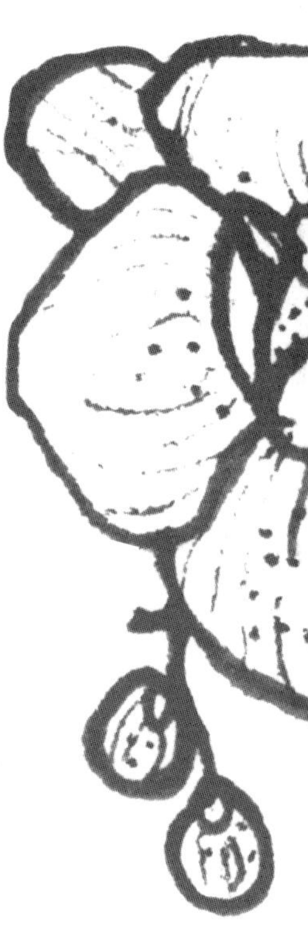

a jaw bone

a stone

like a song you remember singing
in the car when you were young

like the infinite and ending
were the same one

like the land
treasured until it's gone

swallowed by
simmering
rising
seas.

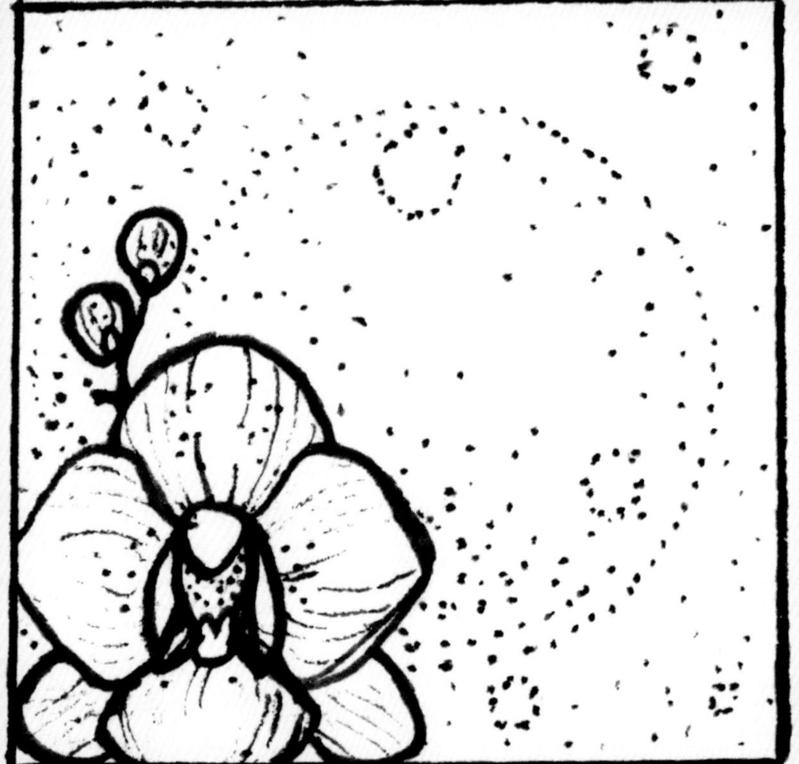

Go Rogue

I latch onto the mantra
let them go
and go off the grid

switch the phone to moon mode
and later switch it off

go rogue
go smoke signals forged in a fire boiling yabbies we caught in the creek

go clouds of white in blue wren open sky backdropping scribbly gums and their scribbly moths frilly wings enchanting

go salt water rock pools with sea foam icing
go strangler fig jutting roots
like benches for the broken

heartbreak will not break me

go snow

go sand under foot

go river pebble paperweight in hand

go back to the land
back to the land
to the land

and let her heal you
when an ending arrives.

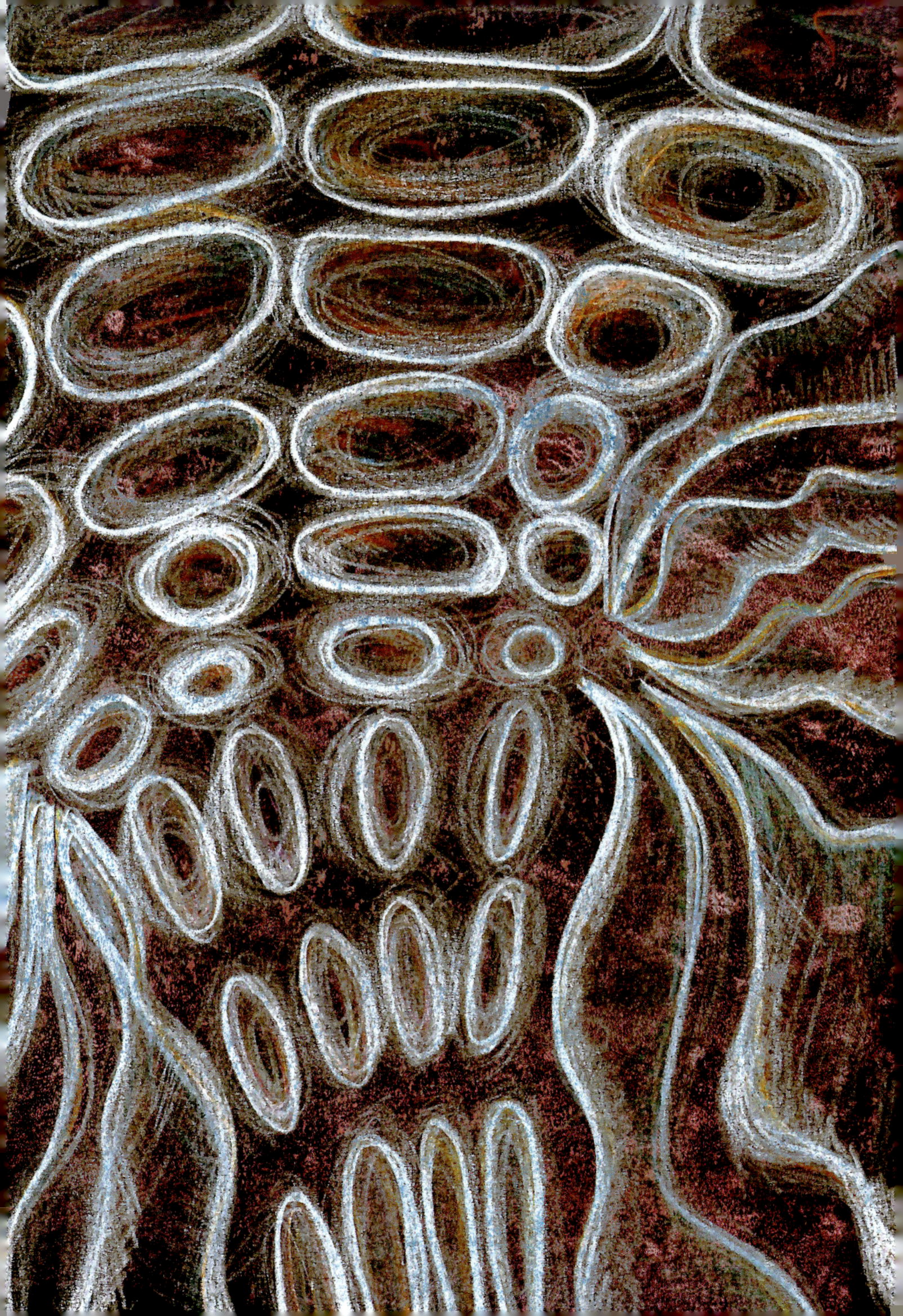

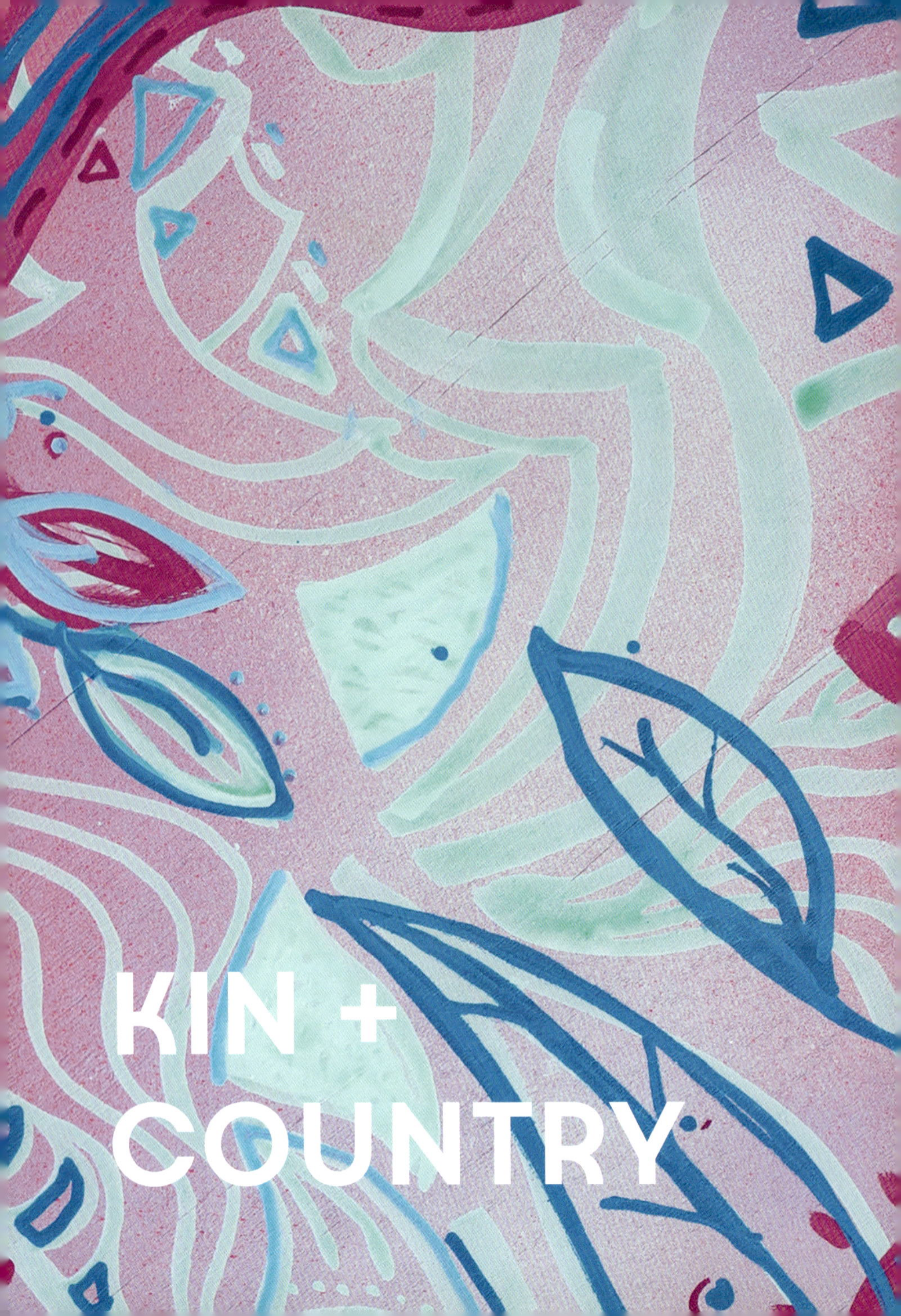

KIN + COUNTRY

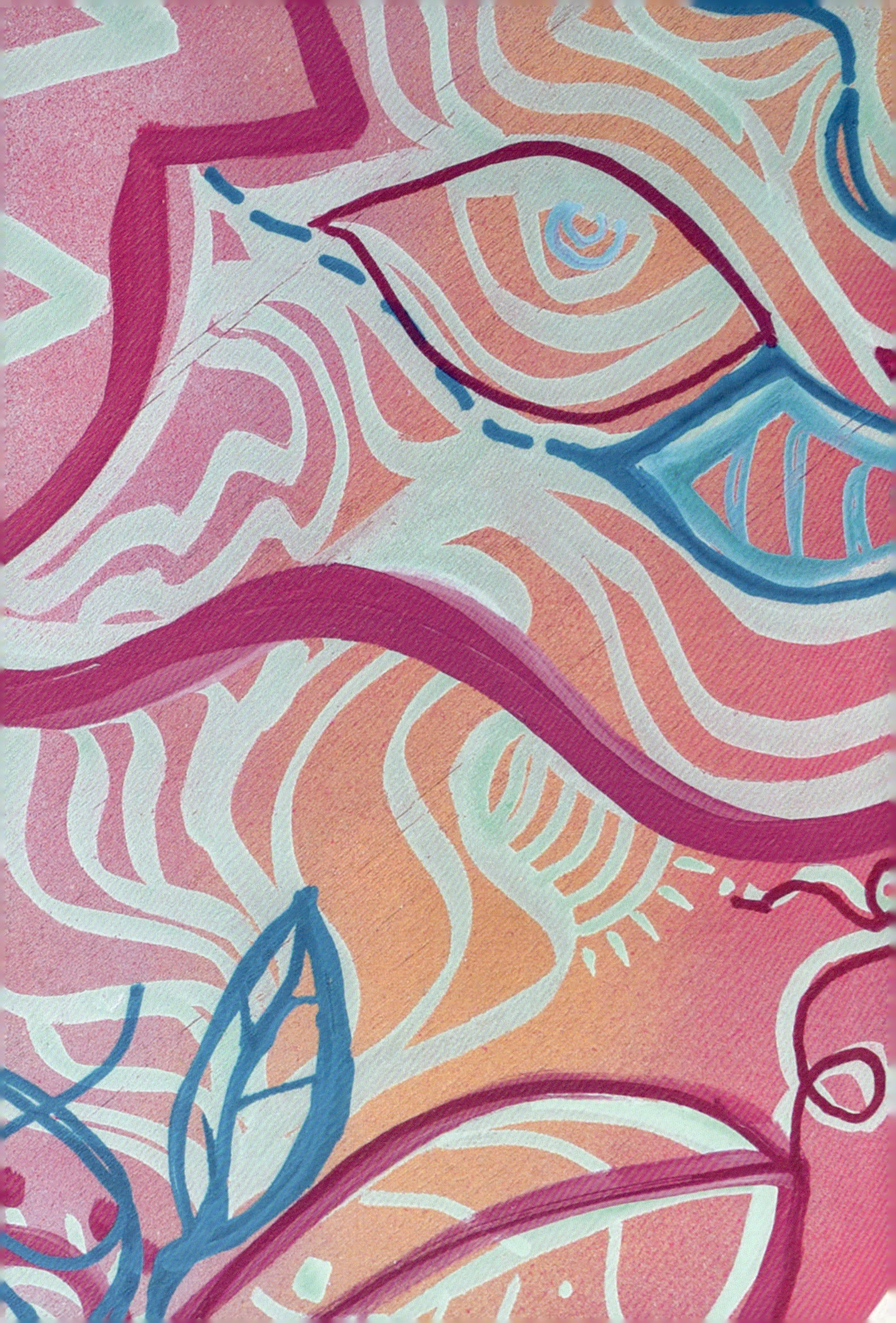

Ngurragu Dhadjam

~ with love and appreciation for the Gumea Dharawal language taught to me by my brother, Ado Webster

ngia ngaradhajāng
dharrabināgen
yindi barraiawulung

yindi yengaga wārri

ya kaiyung gadhu —
warringulwundu ngurra

ya bara yindi
yindi ngurra ballalāng dhadjam?
banna banna nāhway

yindi mirrangia ngalia
wārri dharundharūng

pallanjang ngurra djadjamang yindi ngiagāngguganyala

ngalngia yindi ngiagānggu

buwndj
marraāngga
yindi, ngia, ngurra

kundulali, gambaralānglali, warra, gadhu
yindi ngubudjiāngga

ngalāngga ya naandtha yindi

ngurragu dhadjam

ngurragu dhadjam

ngurragu dhadjam

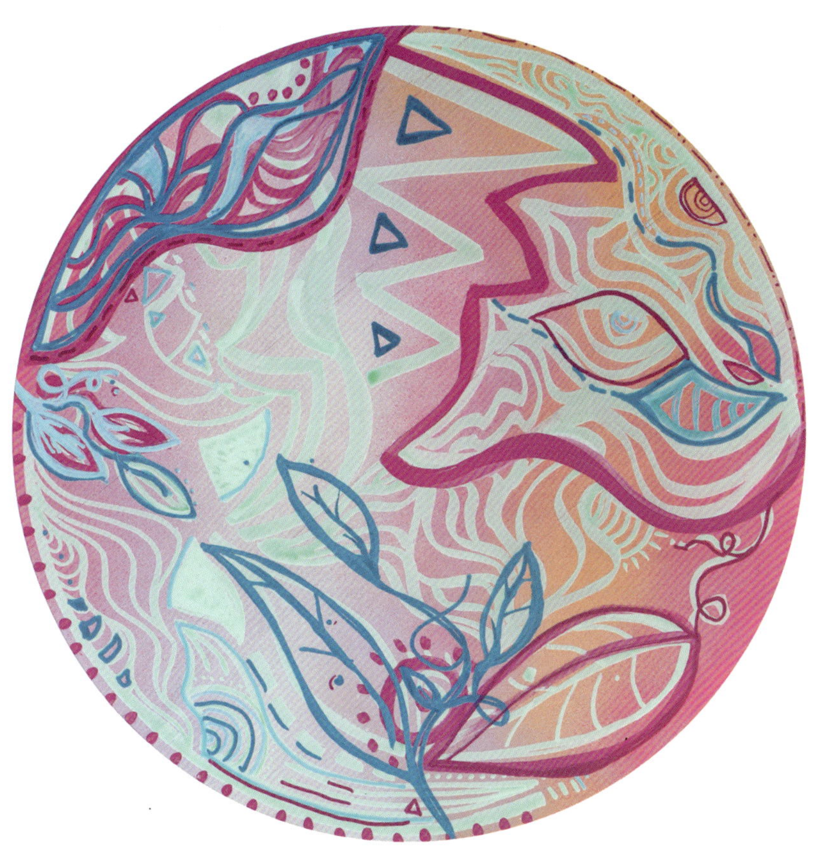

Come Home Soon

I heard the
last rays of sun,
you found them.

You've been gone very long, far far away
to calm seas —
other side of Country

to find *you.*

Will you be homesick soon?
Wet season/big rain (starts) today!

You can't stay
far away always —

saltwater Country/home asks you come towards her.

I want you come towards me too.

Remember
we are kin
you, me, Country.

trees, flowers, mountain, sea
you we love (we love you)

we want to see you

come home soon

come home soon

come home soon

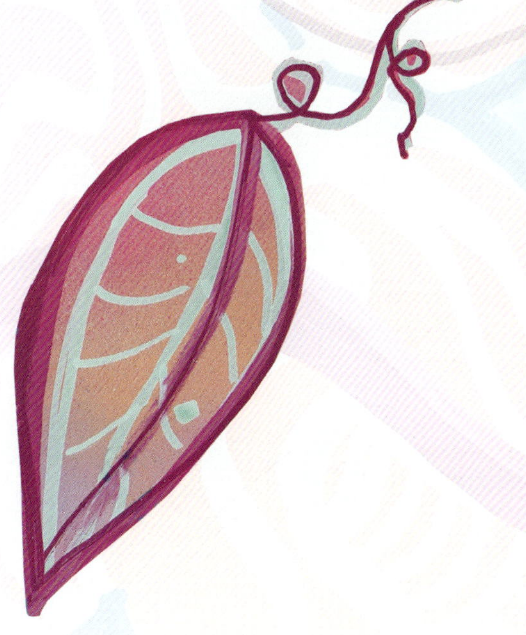

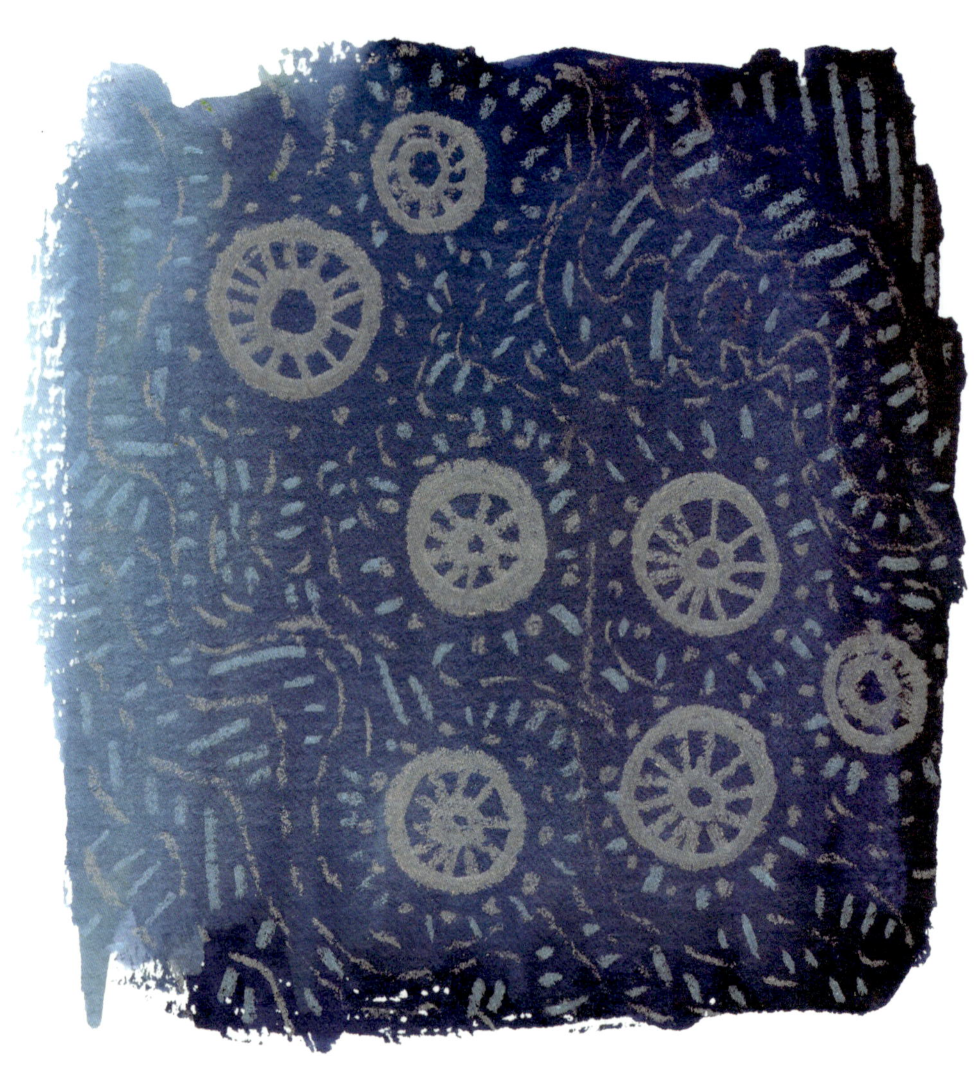

Gugubara | Jerra | Guudhaa

~ For Sam, with thanks to sis, Krystal De Napoli, and all of our Blak astronomers for all times. And with thanks to the Gundungurra people, for holding and sharing celestial stories of the skies that are referenced herein

On the day of our new arrival
I call Aunt
to tell her about the gugubara
who have sung our guudhaa in
with laughing songs

those same birds —
banded in blue
she tells me —
have roused Grandfather Sun
and laid him to sleep
each day
for all times

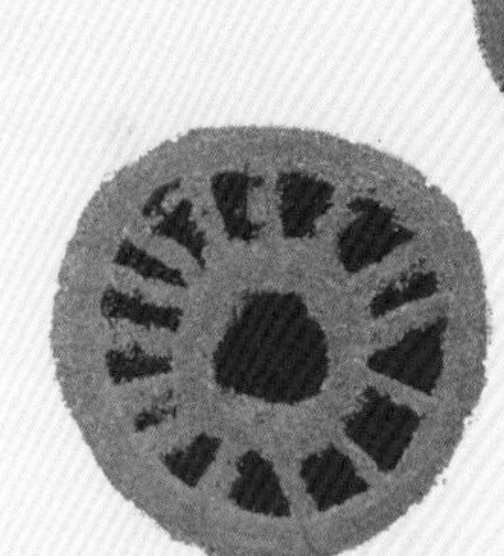

those same birds
remind us to always
see the brighter side.

They roost
as Old Grandfather Sun
wise and warm
returns to camp

and when he does,
Aunt says,

gugubara – kookaburra (Gundungurra)
guudhaa – baby (Gundungurra)

we can see
the seven sisters
as they leap from Mother Earth
to Father Sky

except one
who chooses to stay behind —
down here with us all.

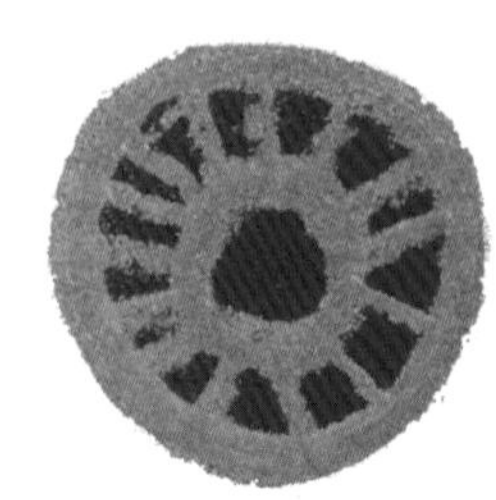

I wonder about this
grounded luminosity

with magnitude marred
by staying here

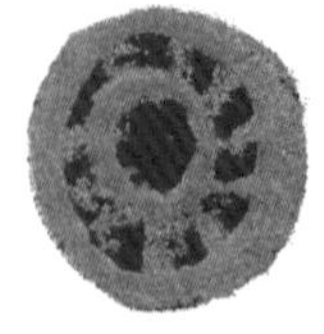

I hope she is
at peace with her landing

picture her dimming and glowing
as the others flow into distant realms

calm, as she knows
that all that she loves

will soon return

when Gugubara sound
and our Grandfather begins to rise
high into the sky

and the variable lights
of the night
find their place
back home

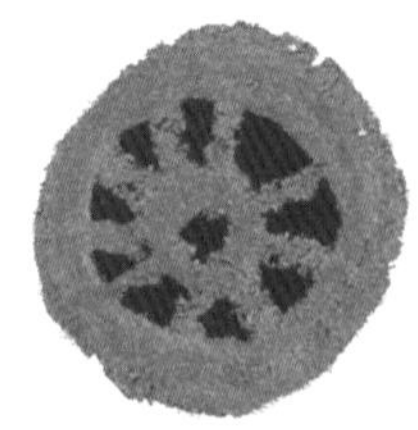

and the guudhaa
who were once the Gugubara
that called jerra back
are returned
to the earthly arms
of their own.

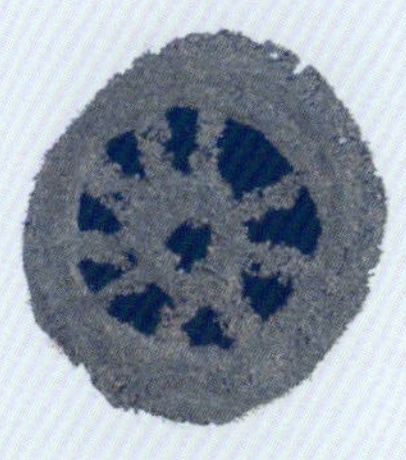

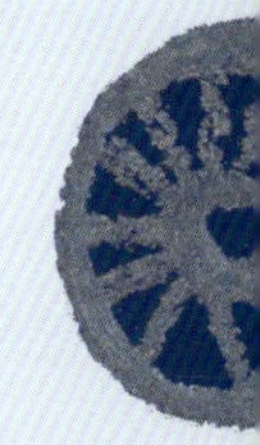

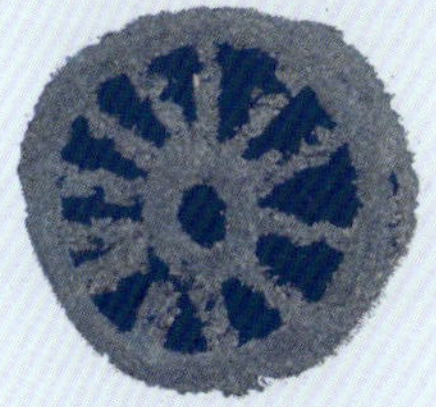

jerra/dyirra – star (Gundungurra)

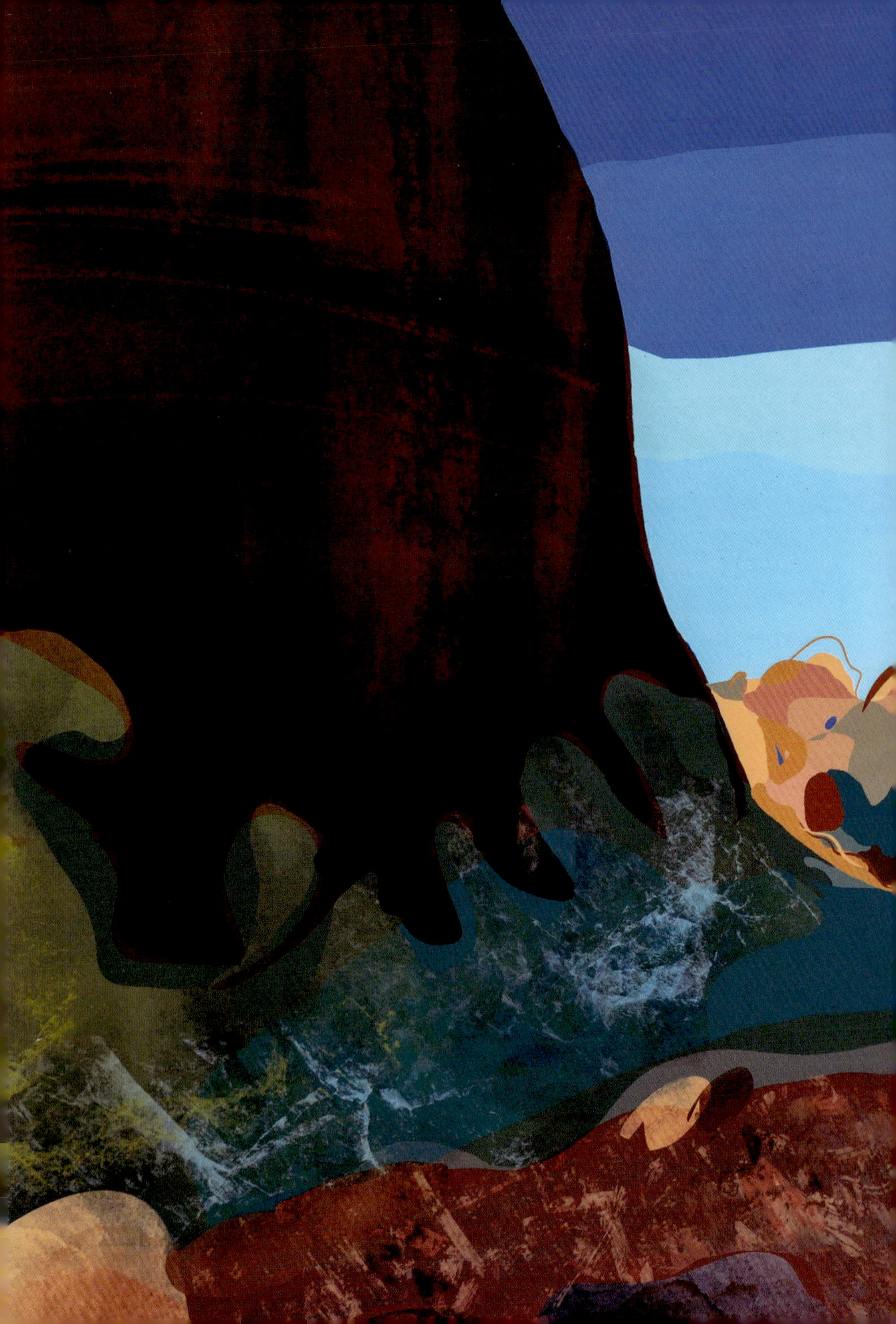

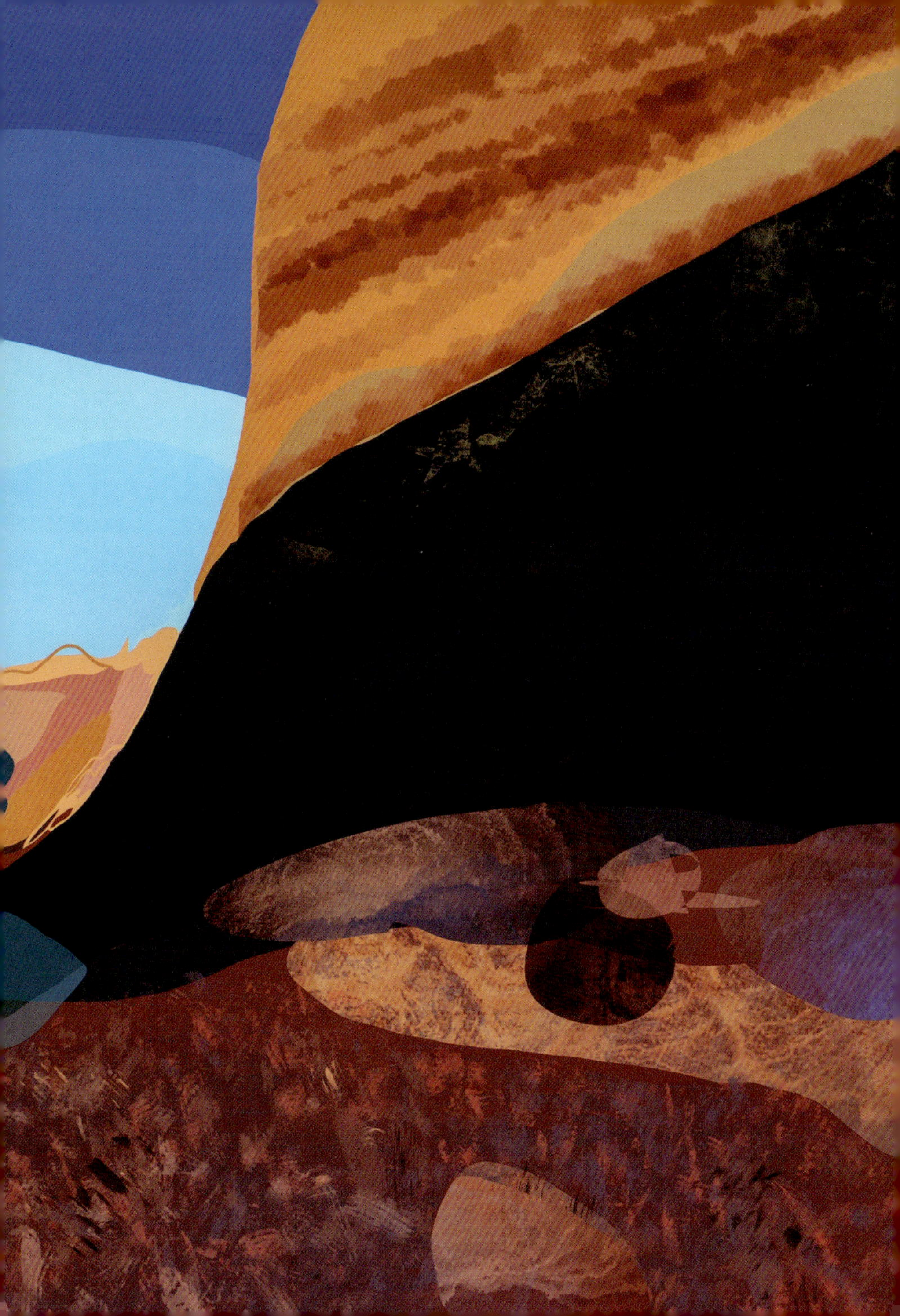

Kinship Country

~ Written with deep thanks and respect for the Elders, families and land that generously held me as I journeyed on Anangu I Pitjantjatjara I Yankunytjatjara I Alyawarre I Arrernte Country

Claustrophobic without the coast, I worry that desert Country
far from salt and sea might landlock me

but she opens with vast

plains
and vocal cords
like winter

o
w
fl er

she sings in —

Anangu | Pitjantjatjara | Yankunytjatjara | Alyawarre | Arrernte

gifts me the word I need
kapi

teaches me to g.a.t.h.e.r. bush food
in sand ..d:u*n:e..
with her bubbies
tells stories in ochre and earth
akin to ours

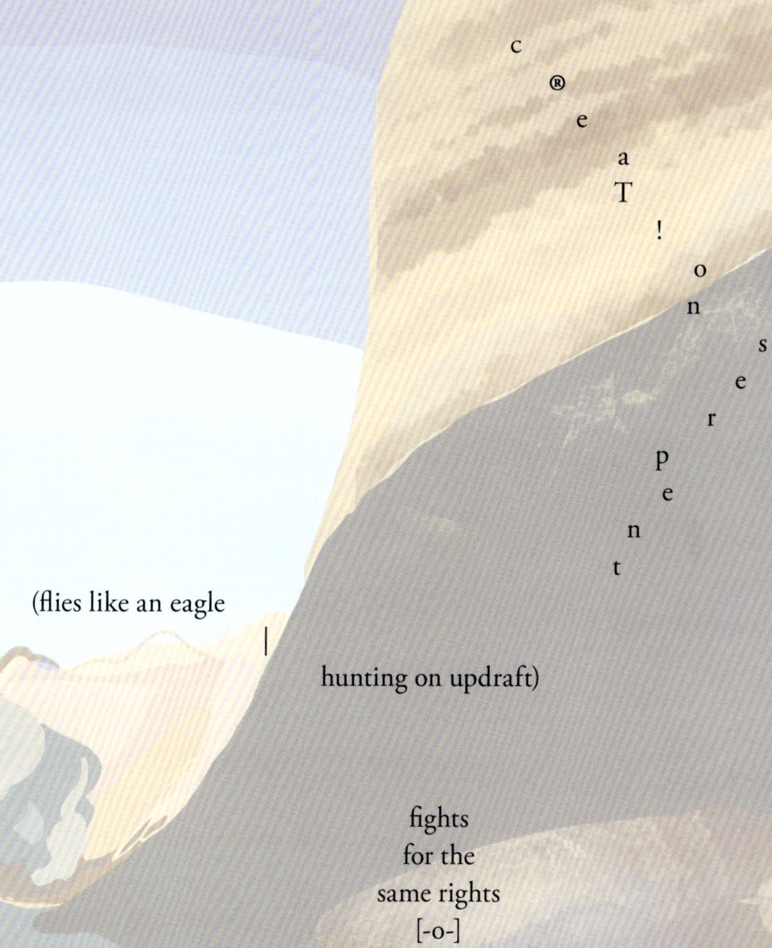

c
®
e
a
T
!
o
n
s
e
r
p
e
n
t

(flies like an eagle
|
hunting on updraft)

fights
for the
same rights
[-o-]

looks at me like my Old People
do over campfire
cooks roo
on coals
sucks the
melting flesh from
vertebrae

she
sips tea
sweet and
blak

from
pannikin

and asks
'when you coming back again?'

I promise

soon

'good' she says

'bring your Mum too'

Calls to Home

~ For Mum

On the hard days
I call my Mother.

Peel back the skin
she grew in her womb
in the shape of me
layer by layer
until I am all heart,

until I am misshapen beat —
erratic and ectopic.

Every time I do,
she holds out her hands
and takes me in them
just as the day I was born.

Over the phoneline
she pulls me to her chest
and reminds me that it is safe to cry
that these are signs of new life —
new chapters.

She hears me when I weep
that I am tired.

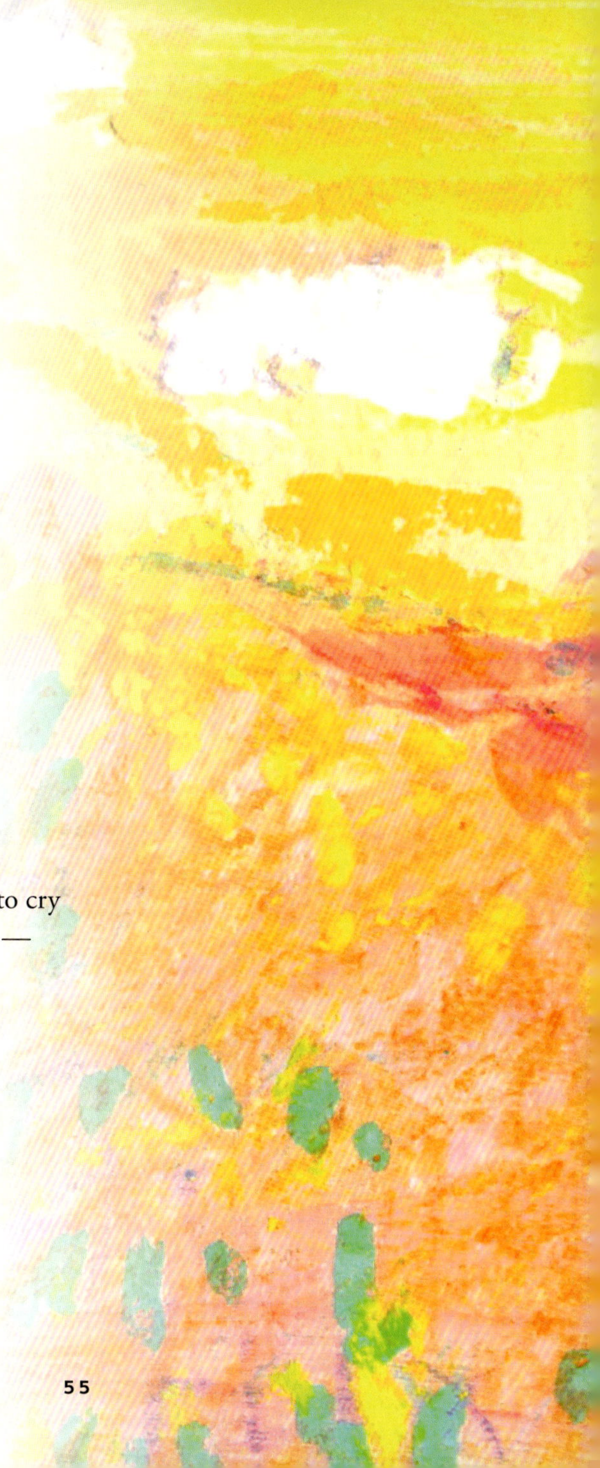

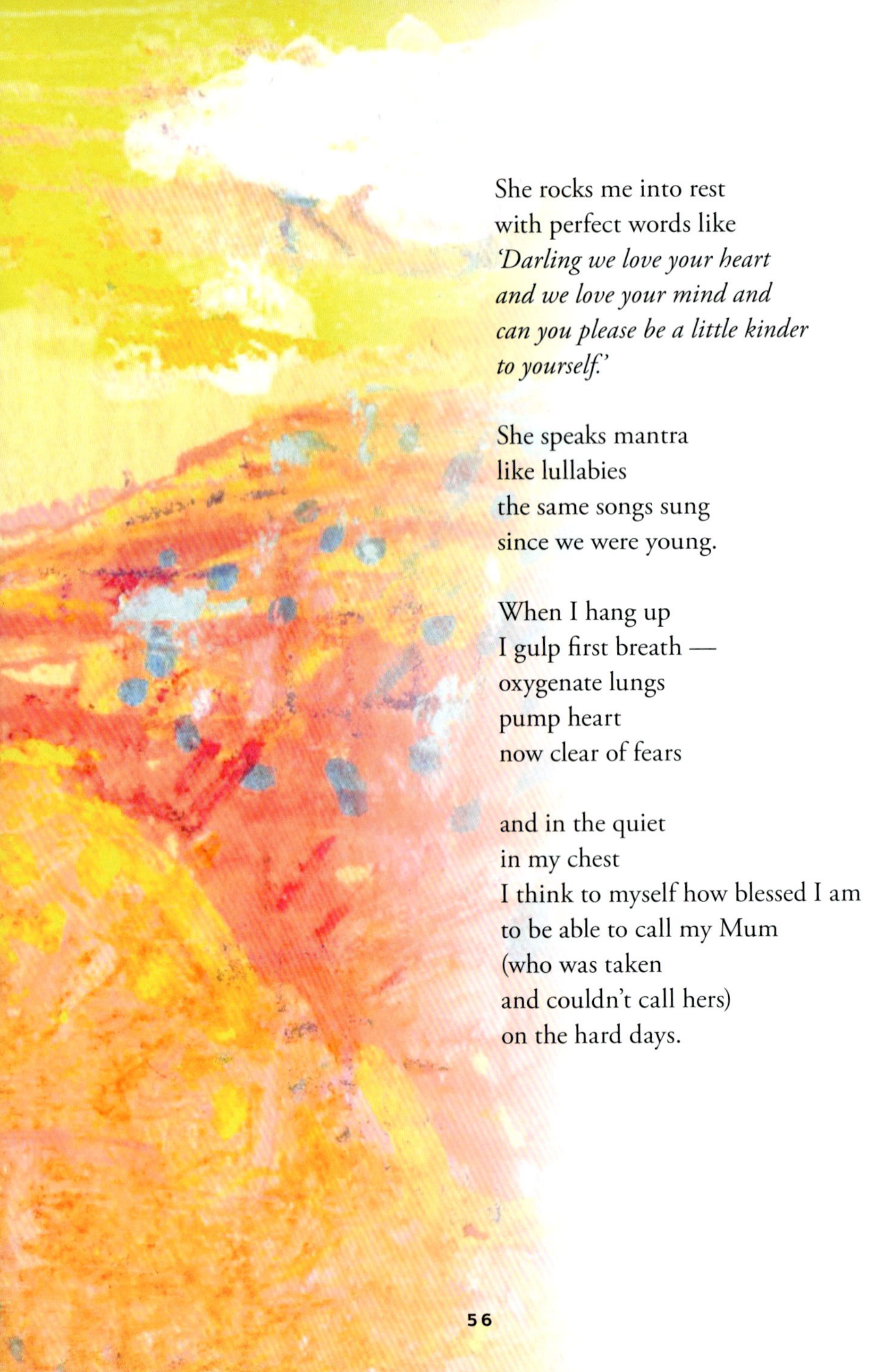

She rocks me into rest
with perfect words like
'Darling we love your heart
and we love your mind and
can you please be a little kinder
to yourself.'

She speaks mantra
like lullabies
the same songs sung
since we were young.

When I hang up
I gulp first breath —
oxygenate lungs
pump heart
now clear of fears

and in the quiet
in my chest
I think to myself how blessed I am
to be able to call my Mum
(who was taken
and couldn't call hers)
on the hard days.

The Falls Trail

~ For Dad

Dad and I walk
the falls track
the same path we've walked
a thousand times
but he is a little older
and so am I
so we walk a little slower

Our dog zigzags ahead
now grey above the eyes
but a pup as he chases birds
and returns at times
as we unpack life

We talk about the past
and its sadness,
the future —
its anxiety,
and find that
in this moment
there is no pain

there is no pain

Dad clears a space
for my worries
as we walk astride.
He holds them
in arms wide
just as we have always done

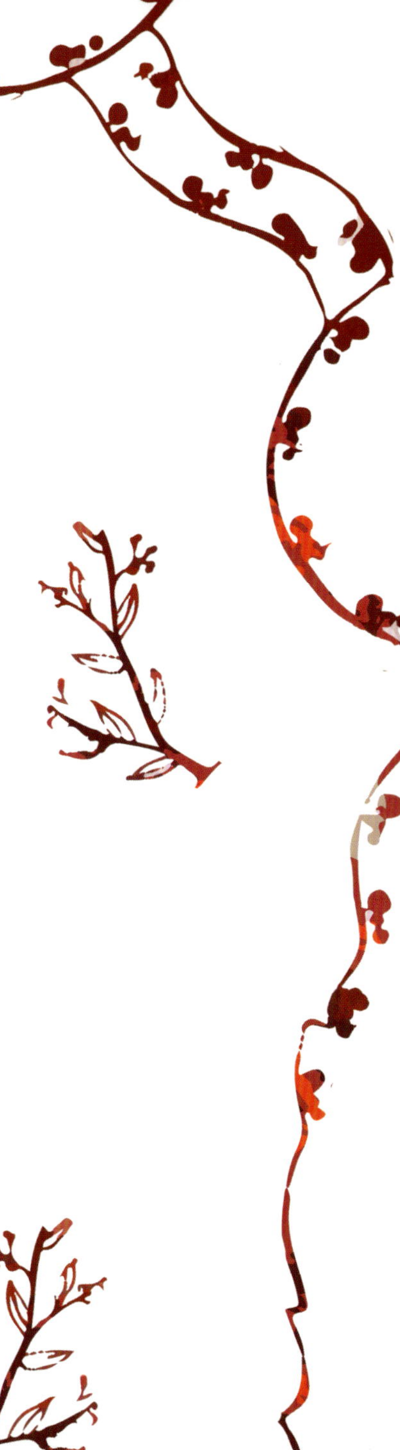

and then he takes my hand
and walks me through them
one by one

On the way back
I tread a little lighter —
freer
for having just talked away the aches
with someone wiser.

We have walked this track
a thousand times
and he is a little older
and so am I
so we walk a little slower
our dog zigzags ahead
now grey above the eyes
and with a spirit and mind undone,
I find new space to worry
about a day
when I can't
cast these thoughts away
on a walk down the Falls Trail
with my Dad.

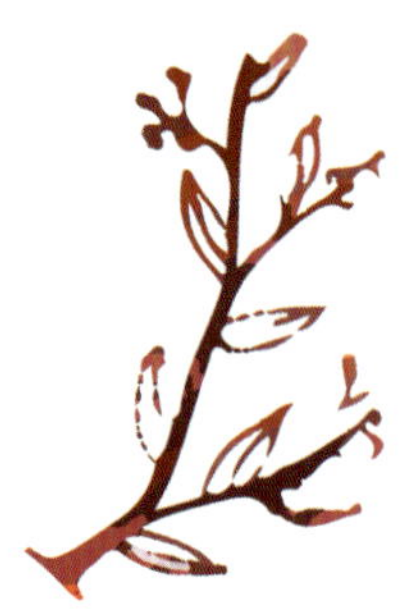

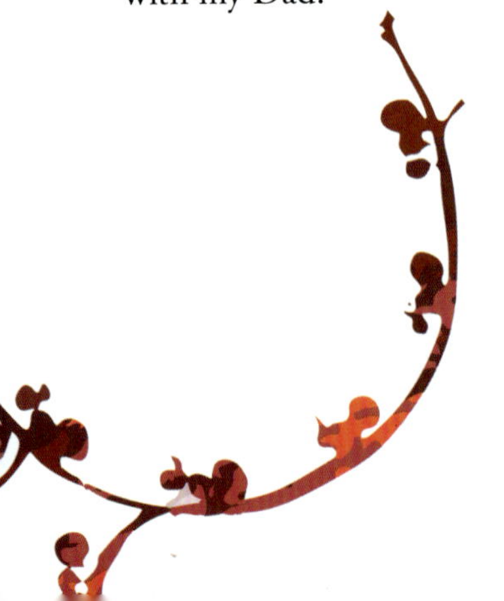

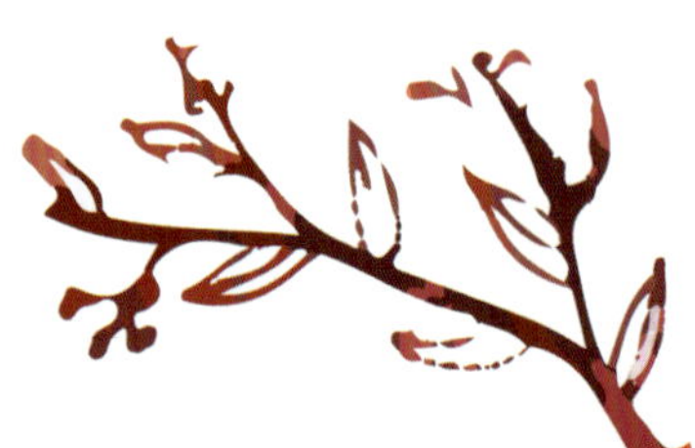

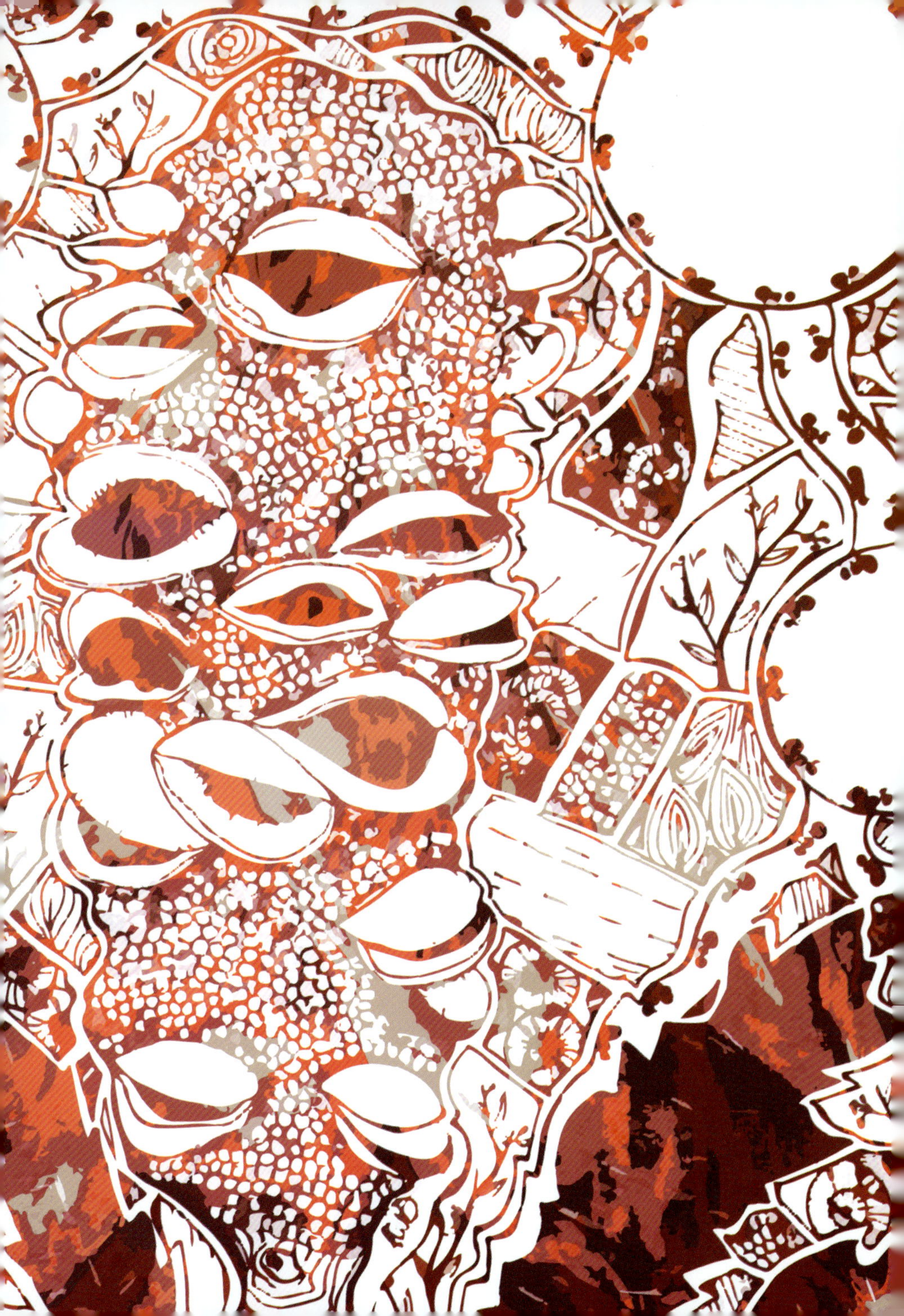

Sacred Women Ways

~ For our Matriarchs and theirs

I remember the day we met
I eyed you shyly
unsure of how your magic might arrive

I watched it fly right by me
pulling me in to a safe place of growth
and you showed me how to go
the *Old Way*
slowly and kind

since, I've been trying to do the same
for our *young ones*
to channel those *Sacred Women's Ways*
as you do
you know the way

you always knew the way

to stay just as bold and grounded
to follow guidance
to hone defiance
for anything less than what's best
for our people

in the process of my becoming
I've been blessed to learn from you
and your teachers —
present in all that you do
anew with the actions of now.

young women
on the move for justice
speaking truths out loudly
hearts proudly alight with fires
lit by Ancestors fighting for rights
your embers still warm us now

and like them
when you're gone
we'll carry your song

and we promise
with your Old Ways magic
to always sing along.

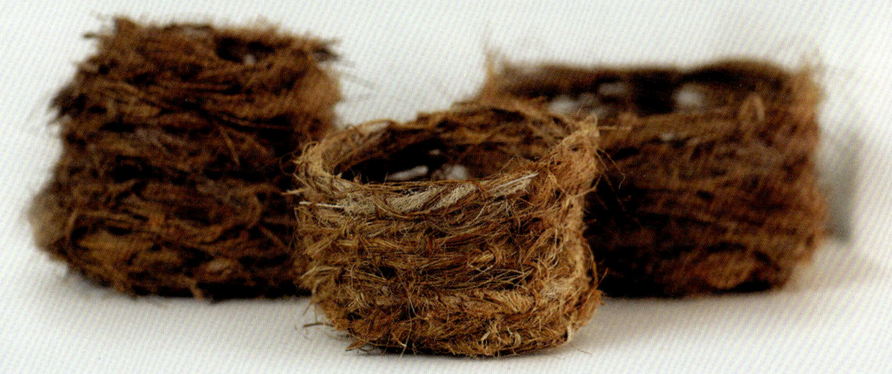

Black is Beautiful

~ With thanks to Ziggy Ramo and his iconic Black Thoughts album and after Sonya Renee Taylor, who taught me that *'the body is not an apology'*

They didn't have Aunty or Sister Girl,
on the cover of Vogue

Marie Claire and Vanity Fair
fronted models
with straight hair
and skin lighter than mine

crisped in tanning tanks to acquire
our melanin-dipped limbs
while denying
the racism we faced
behind the scenes

they had visible ribs
botox lips
overnight nose jobs
and tummies that got sucked in
and then tucked
as they aged

no stretch marks

no greys

everything monetised to beautify

Tide gone out
skinny ankles meander
through rocky outcrops
where Young Uncles
teach nephies how to
pocket-knife shuck
delicate oysters for family

full-breasted Mums nurse
chubby bubs
on near-ripe pigface-laced sand

everywhere
juicy brown lips
part for Earth's generous gifts
chins meet sun

saltwater sustenance
becomes human

afternoon clouds blush
at young ones who paint
themselves
with ochre

sea spray carries away their giggles

wax and peroxide
to bleach and pluck

lipo and dieting
to shuck and drain

everything
not 'beautiful'
away

when it dries
they wash crackled patterns
in shallow waves
cream curdles billow
fogging Nanny's wade nearby with
earthy art, she

twists and sways | twists and sways
teaching her littles
to dance for bangajaang, entranced
everywhere they look
they see that
Black is beautiful.

bangajaang – pipi (Gumea Dharawal/Dhurga)

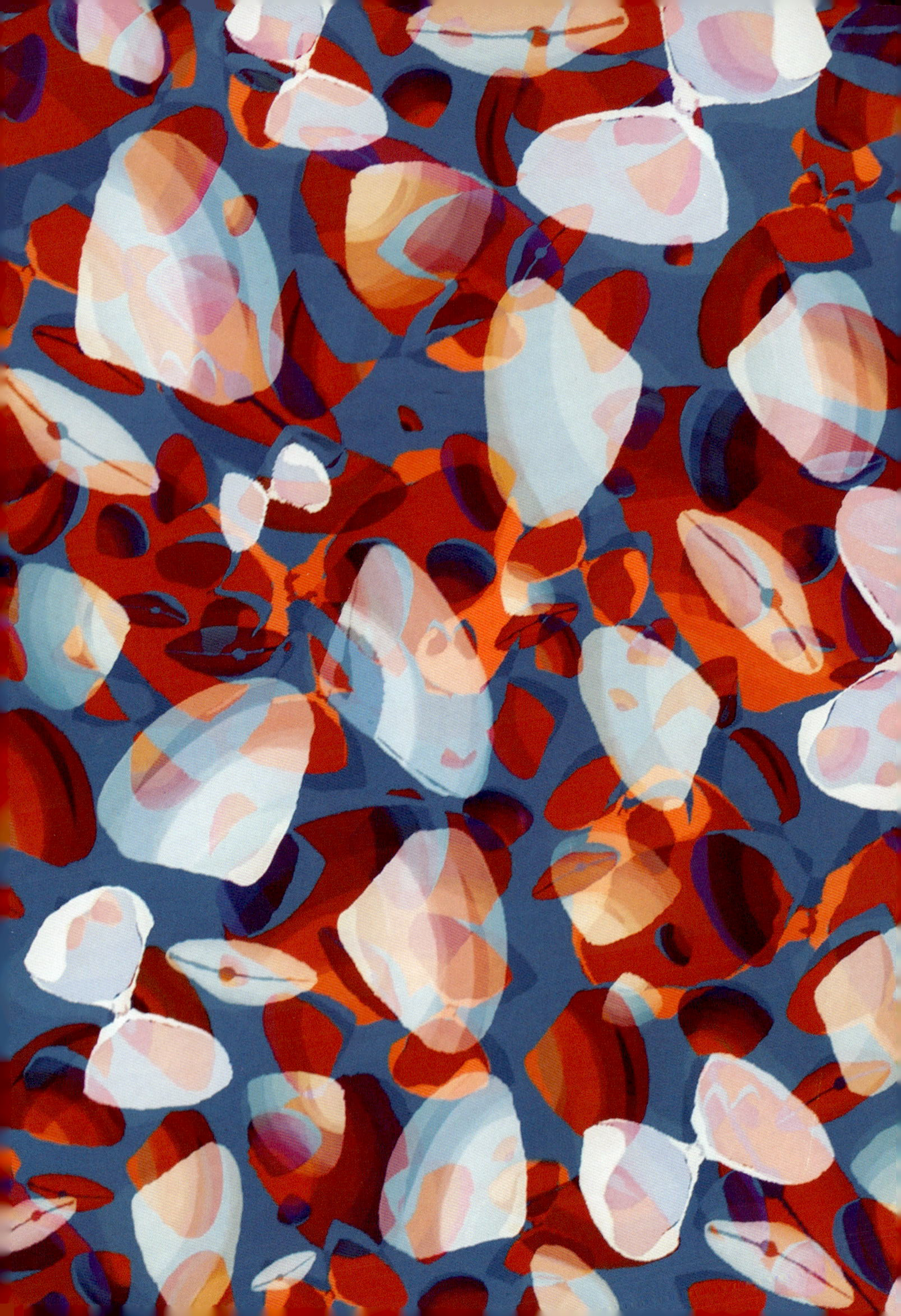

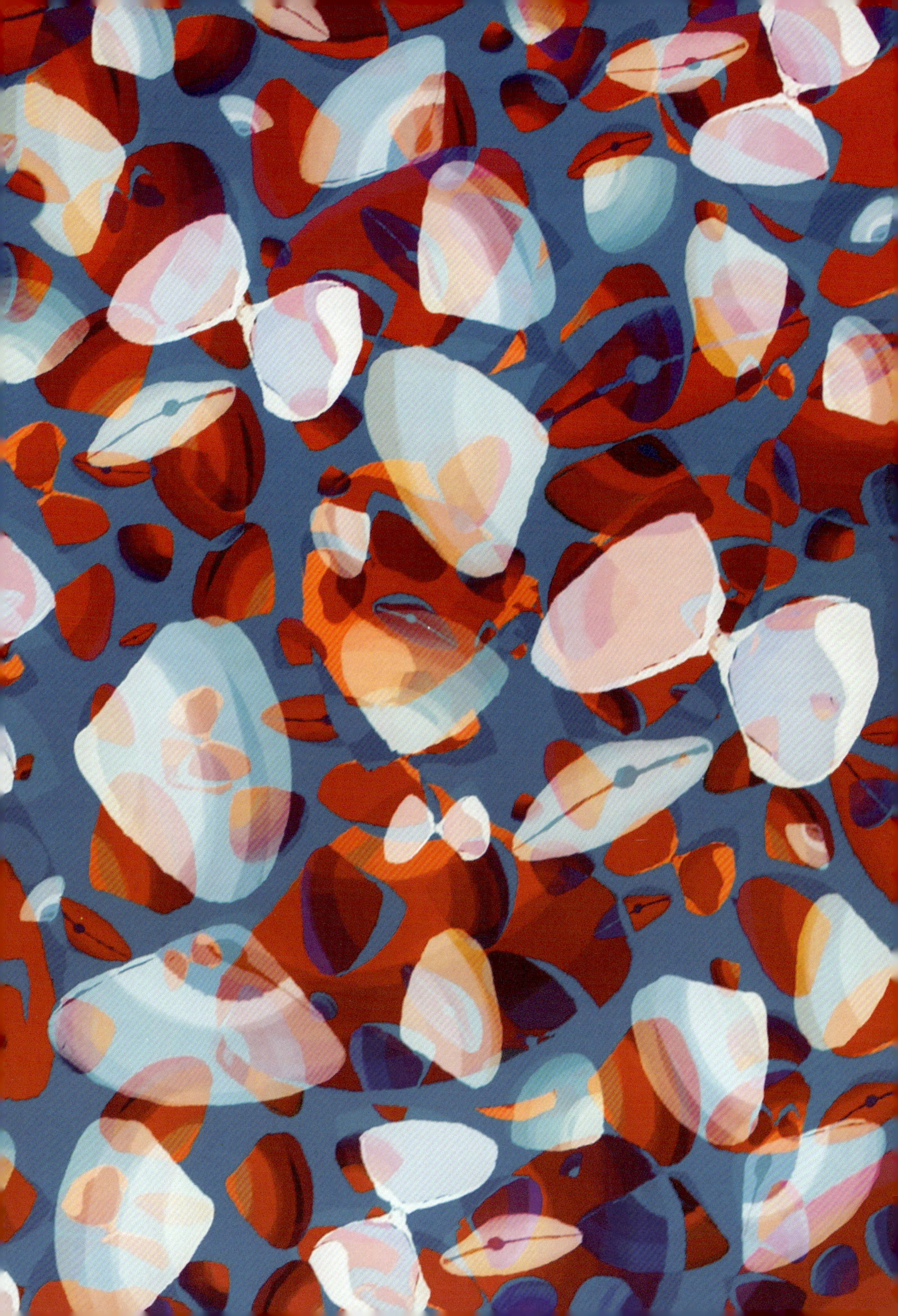

Sea Eagles

~ Written on the Ngangbul,
Bundjalung and Arakwal lands
with gratitude for the Aunties

Aunty tells me
'*bub, the women here*
don't follow the rules

and you don't have to either.'

She tells me Creation story

how the matriarch
made the waves.

Above her movement,
I watch another mother's
fledglings
finding strength
in newly formed
feathers.

I hope that
like theirs
mine will grow here too
and carry me nimbly.

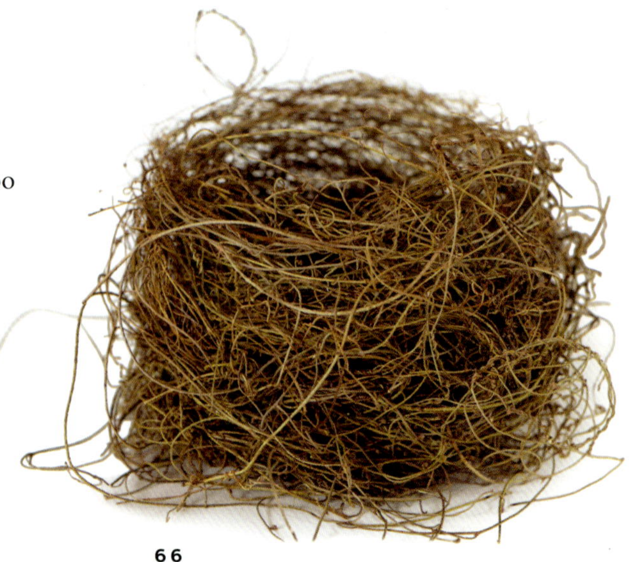

Blooming

~ For my Ancestors, and family,
and for Minyama Waratah,
the home that raised us on
Gundungurra Country

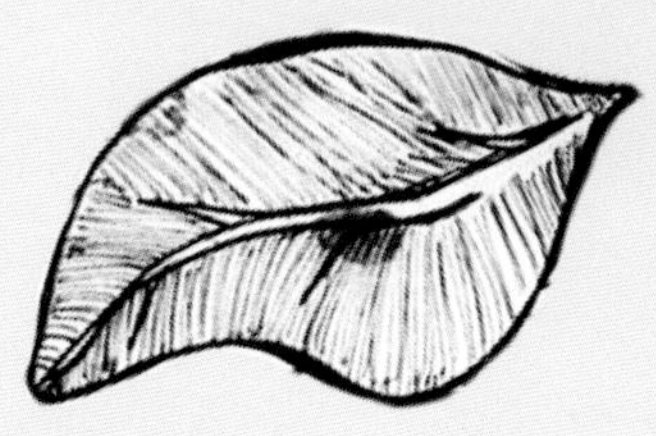

When Home calls
I scale the escarpment

brace myself for the arms
of kin that will catch me

by blooming
waratahs —

Country's red heart

and totem

who've withstood
drought
and climate change

estranged from
resistance
other spirits have met

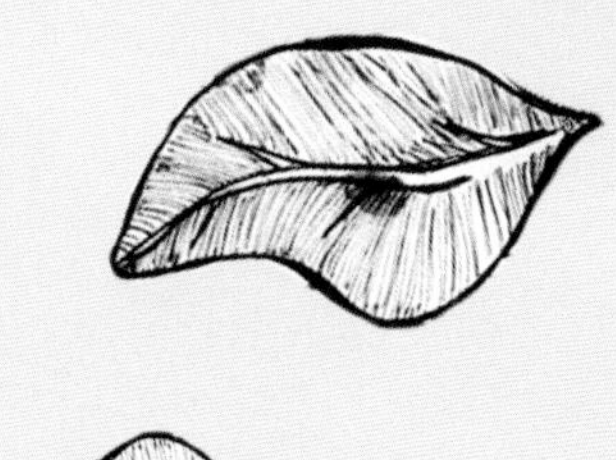

persistent on
opening up
each year.

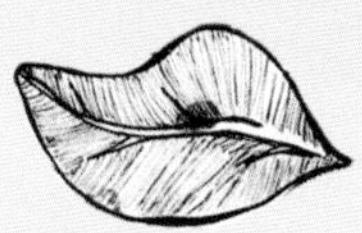

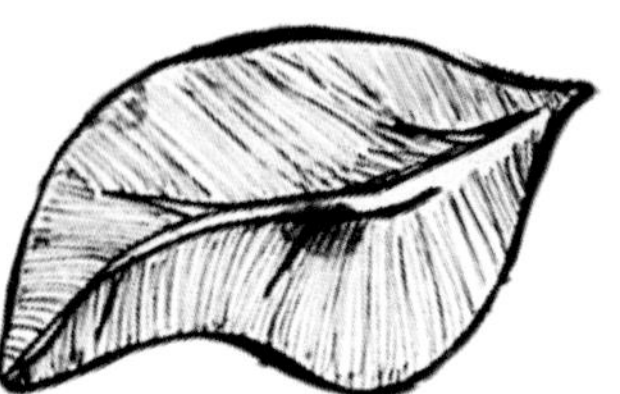

Here the Ancestors
speak in flowers

and we've been gifted
the power

to understand.

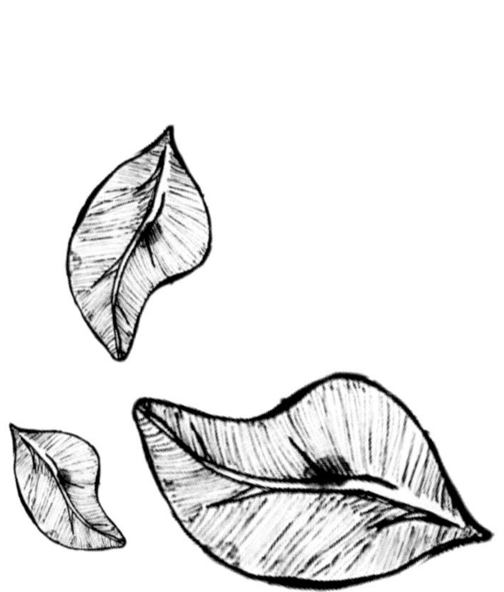

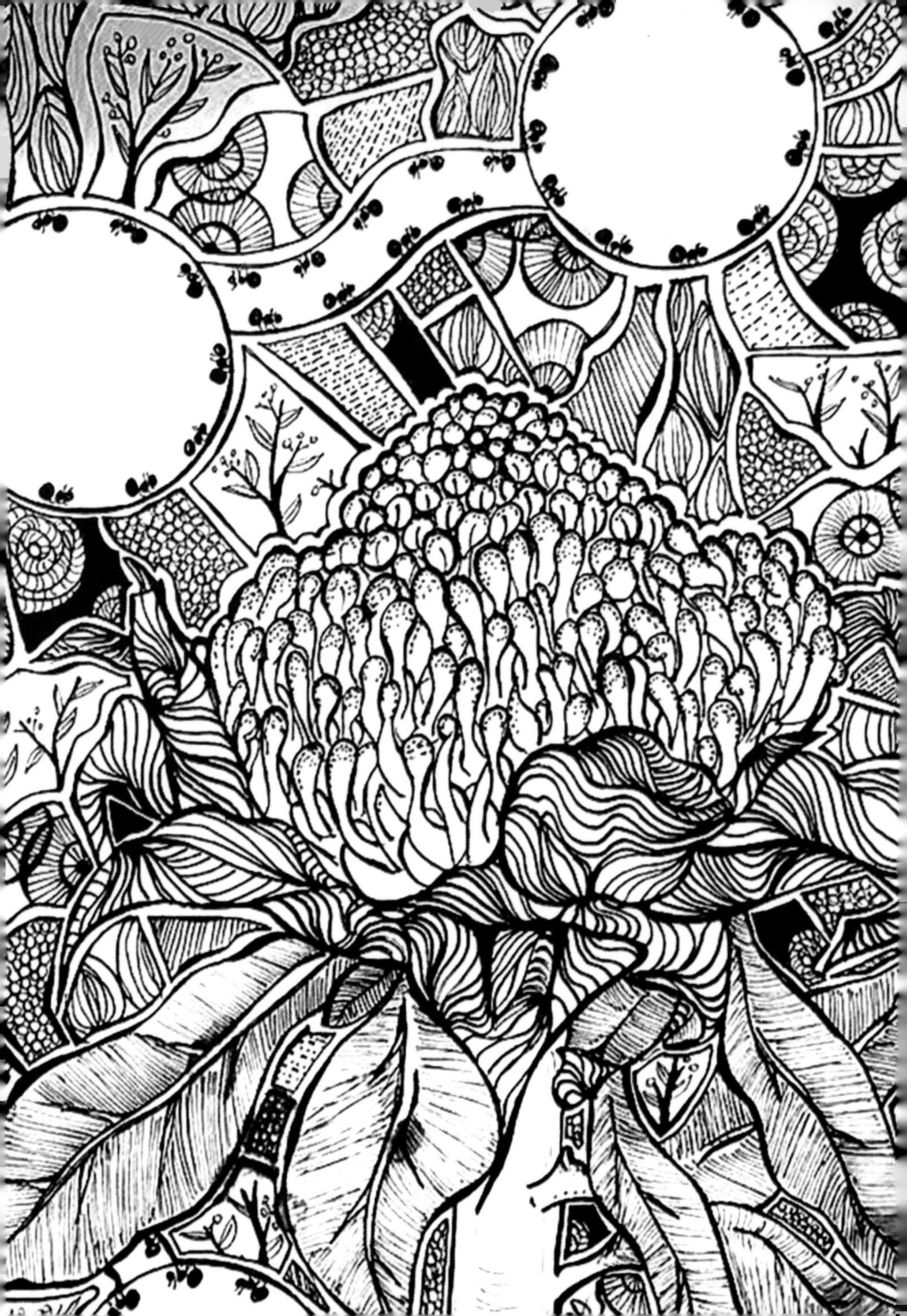

Aftermath

When my world
burns down around me

I take the cold ash
and crush it

between my fingers and thumb

I roll it in my upturned palm —
a shaking hand whisking
back and forth

for the misguided beliefs
that landed as thoughts
and manifested action
which led to this inferno

I empty, seeing the black dust stains
stick to skin
as a reminder
of creative destruction

I bend
to the ashen rubble
on the earth

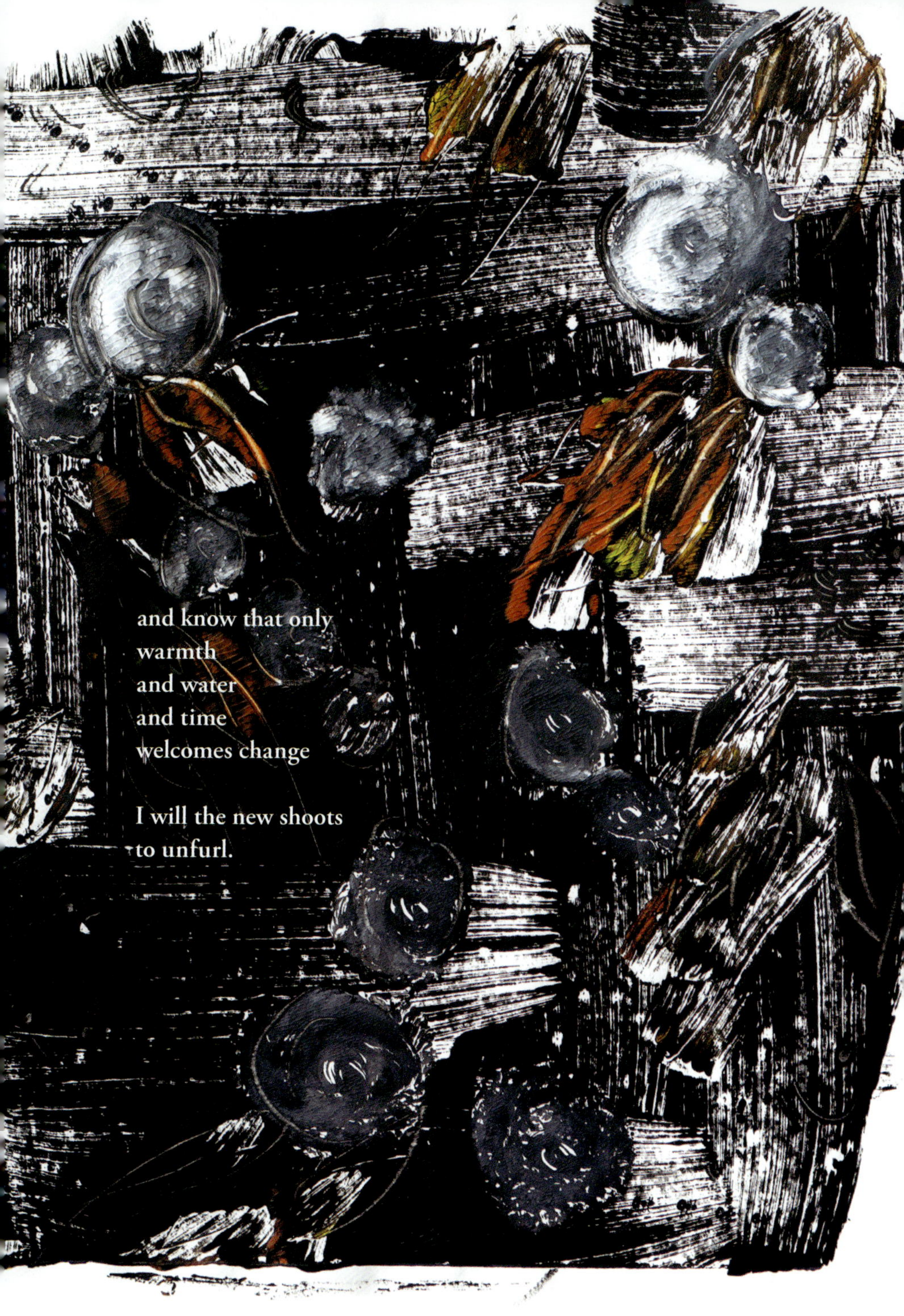

and know that only
warmth
and water
and time
welcomes change

I will the new shoots
to unfurl.

Messengers

~ For the birds, may their spirits return to the Dreaming and after Robin Wall Kimmerer, who taught us *'To love a place is not enough. We must find ways to heal it'.*

I found five of our messengers
shot

their bodies
laid amongst kelp wreaths

sand and microplastic
infesting organs

fly-bitten eyes
sealed shut

beaks bent
to cease
transmission

too little too late.

Yet loud and clear
I received

their call:

our world
is burning

temperatures
are rising

the birds
are dying

at the hands
of greed.

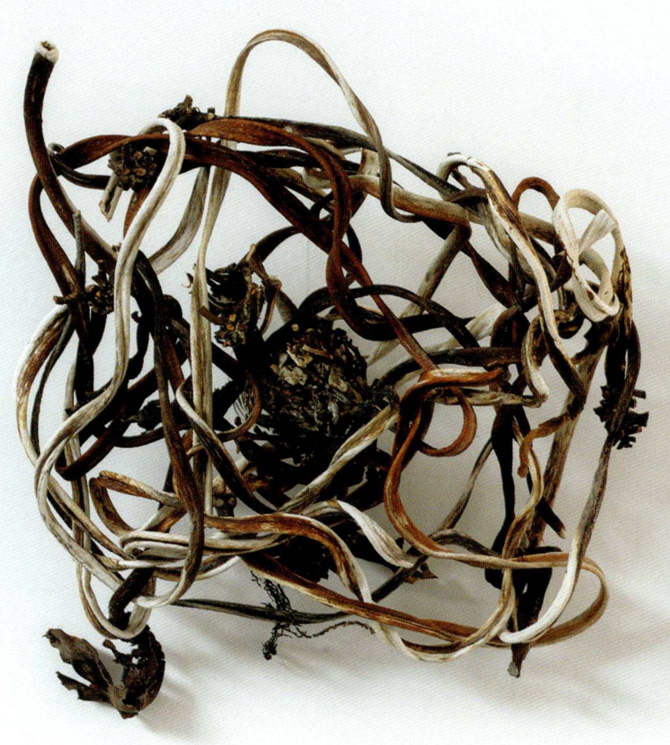

Sky Lessons

Seeking quintessence.
I look to Father Sky

who doesn't cling to a shape
or question his size

or the forms that adopt him
as the clouds pass by.

I breathe
and bathe
in his vastness

learn it's
not unlike mine

and grounding in this kinship
and presence
I find

that I can remain open
and be as he is

a smattering
of sunsetting colour
holding space
for the stars
as the dark
settles in.

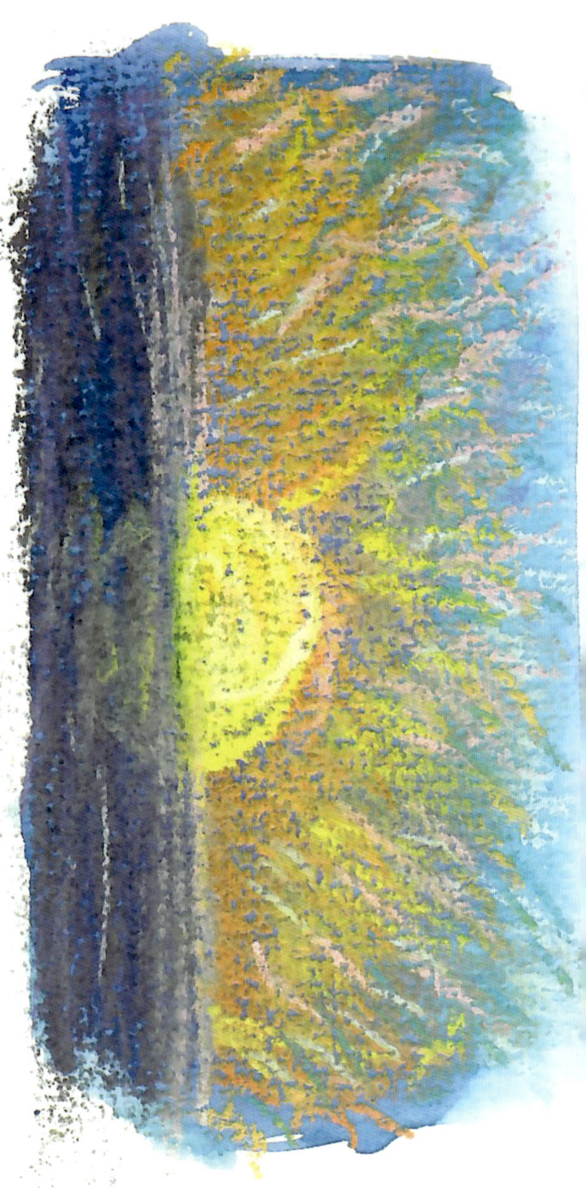

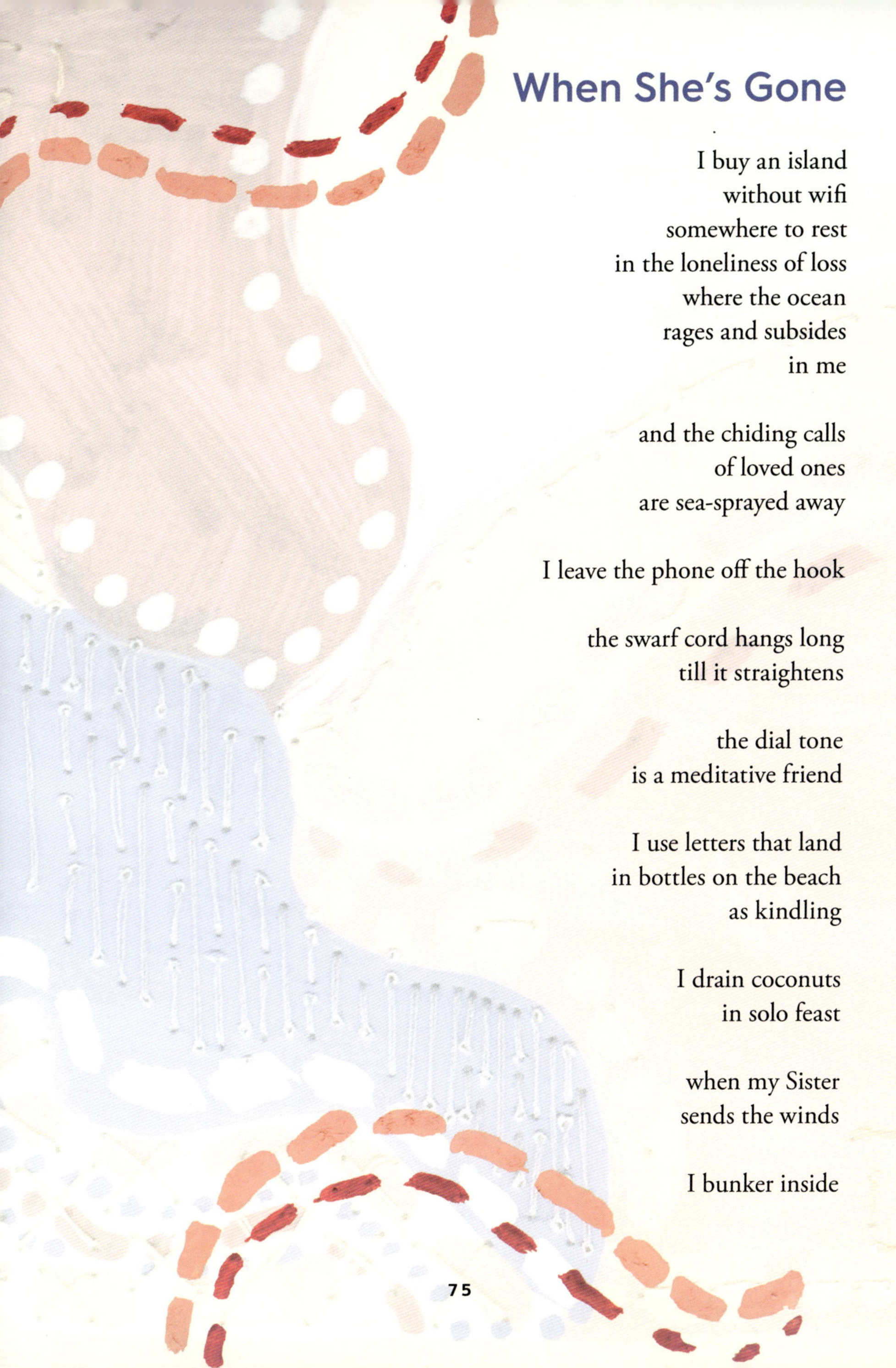

When She's Gone

I buy an island
without wifi
somewhere to rest
in the loneliness of loss
where the ocean
rages and subsides
in me

and the chiding calls
of loved ones
are sea-sprayed away

I leave the phone off the hook

the swarf cord hangs long
till it straightens

the dial tone
is a meditative friend

I use letters that land
in bottles on the beach
as kindling

I drain coconuts
in solo feast

when my Sister
sends the winds

I bunker inside

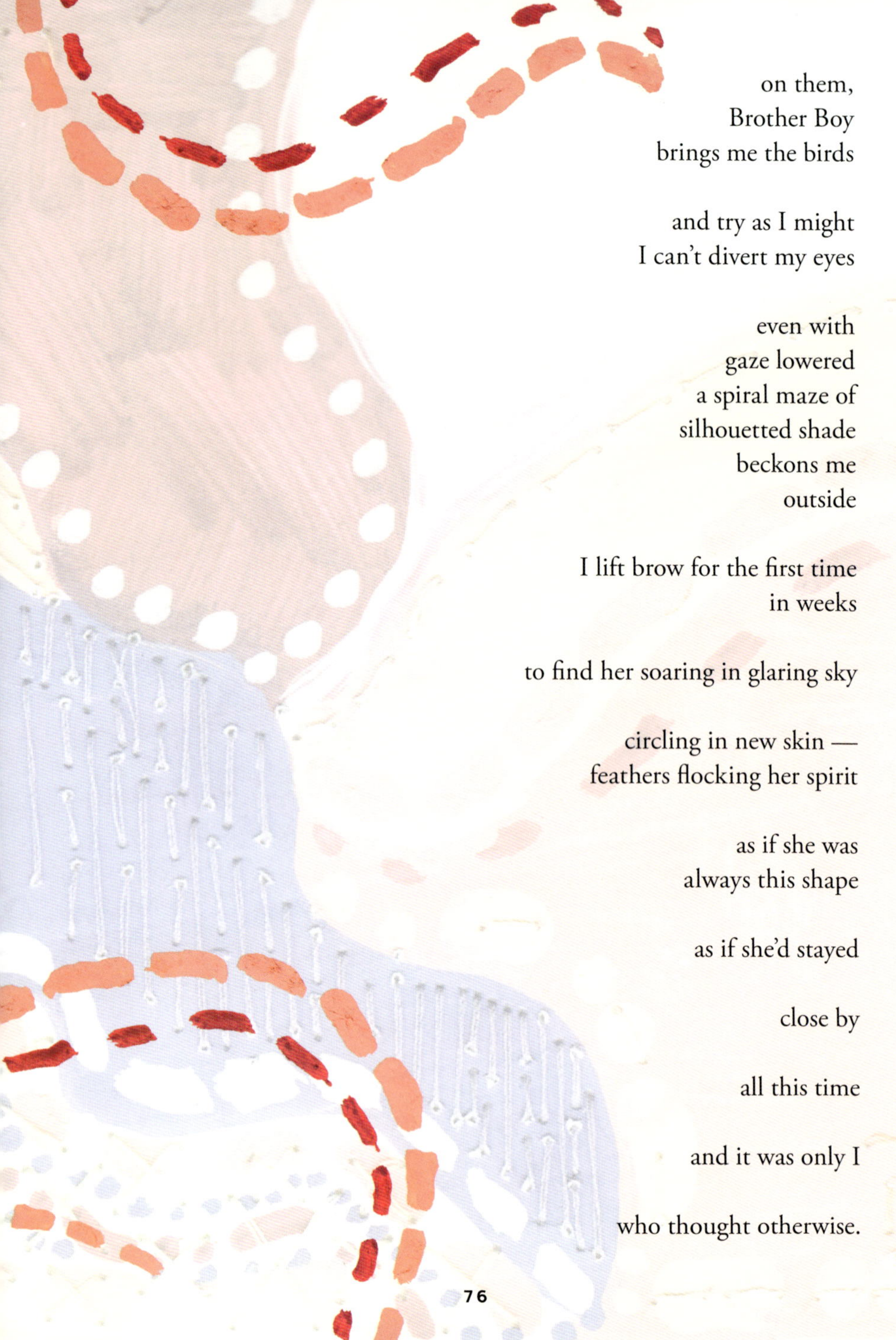

on them,
Brother Boy
brings me the birds

and try as I might
I can't divert my eyes

even with
gaze lowered
a spiral maze of
silhouetted shade
beckons me
outside

I lift brow for the first time
in weeks

to find her soaring in glaring sky

circling in new skin —
feathers flocking her spirit

as if she was
always this shape

as if she'd stayed

close by

all this time

and it was only I

who thought otherwise.

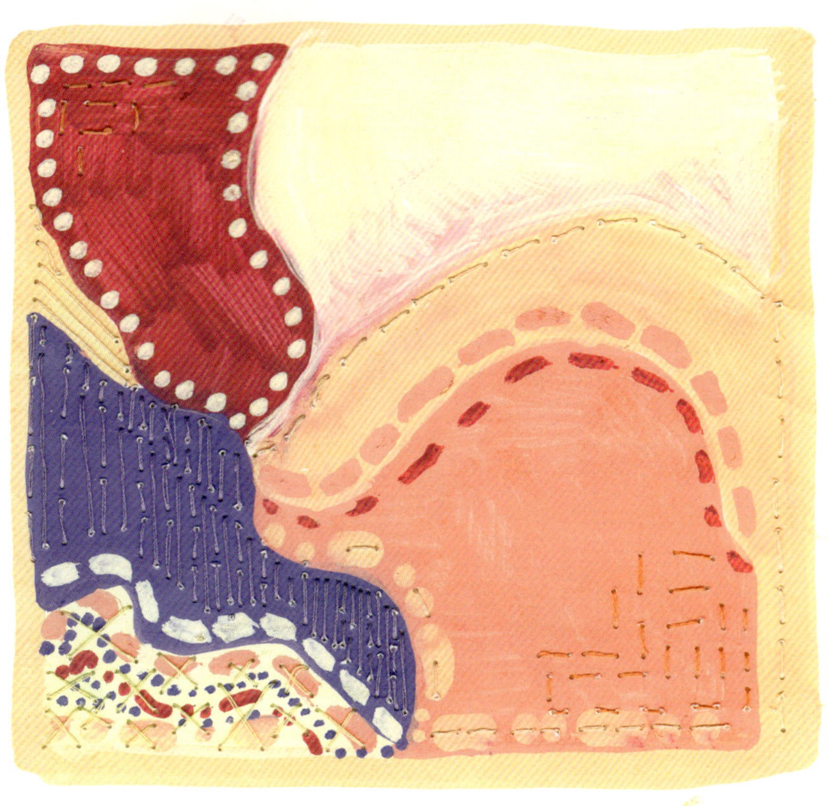

They Sung Us

The Old People rain smiles
for their song
which brought us to be

their glee moves in me
like river mint picked
and crushed on the breeze

magpie gargle and waddle
carefree

like inland pearls
mussel flesh agleam

dewy fresh-cut scar tree

like billy tea
strong, black, sweet

waratah-stained flame
pop-crackle-simmering

eucalyptus smoke
from coolamon
billowing
until we're clean

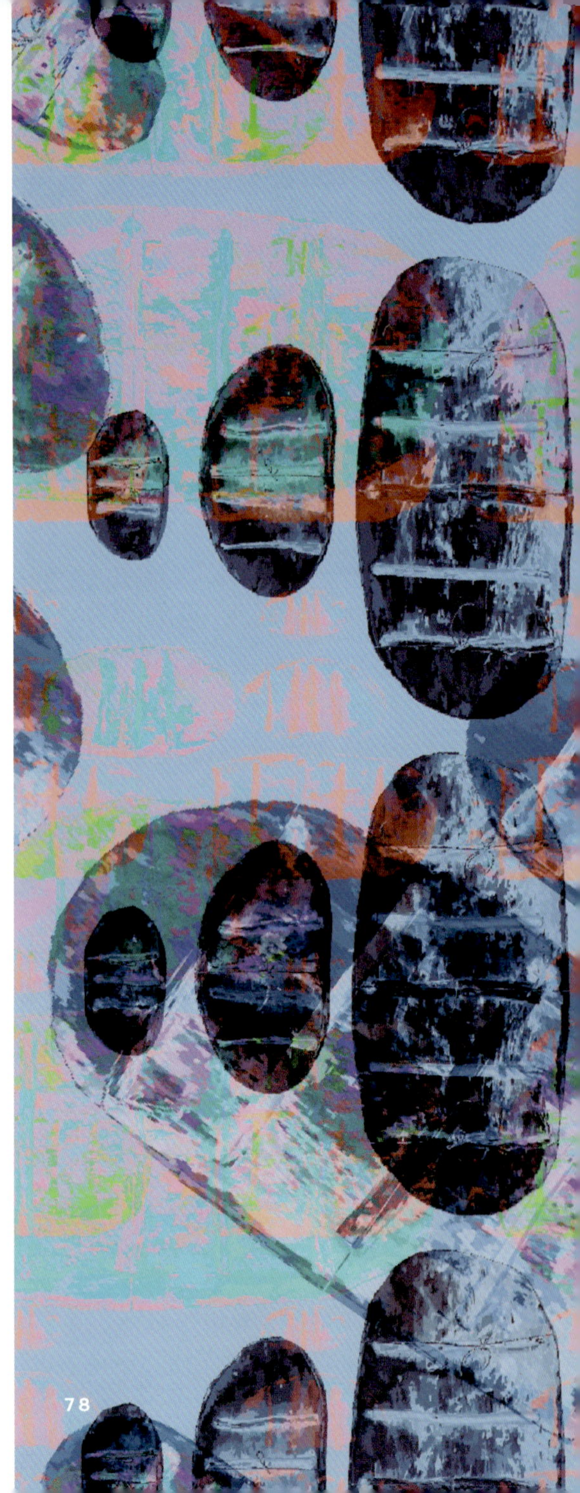

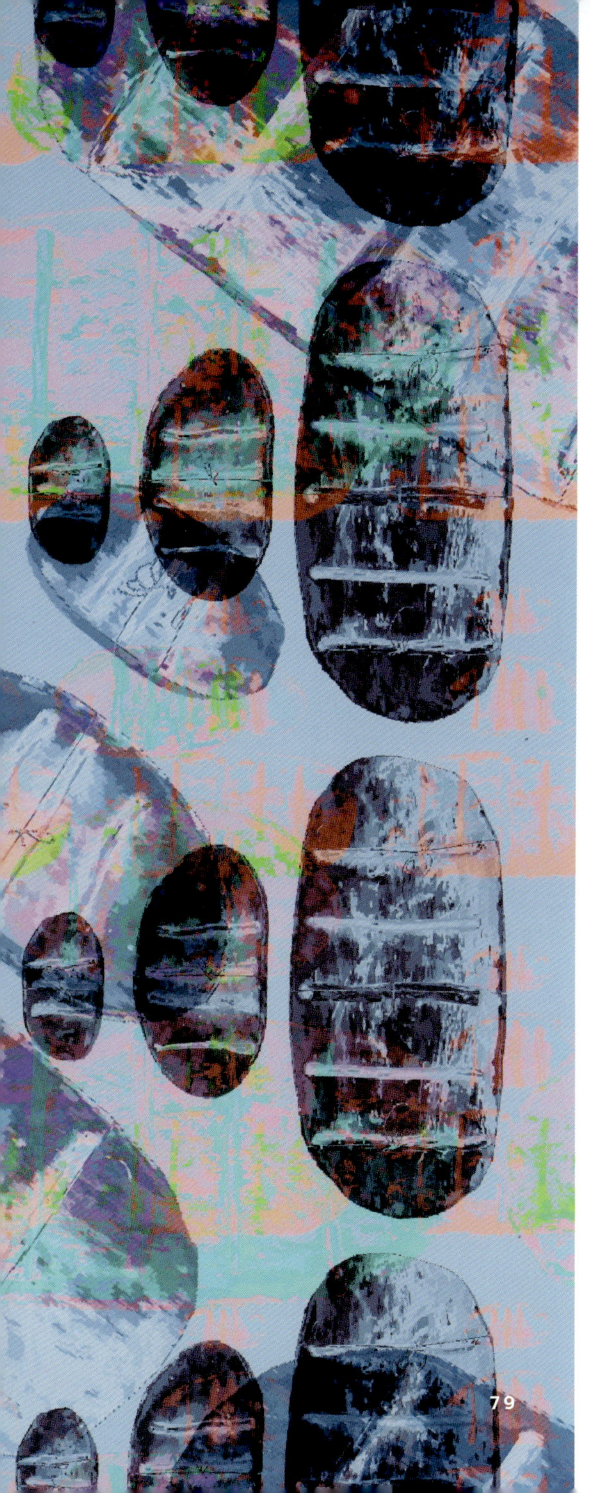

like estuary fish
both upstream,
one with the sea
and her expanse

like full moonbows
guaranteeing
we see

what this means
for us now

and reap what they
sowed when they sung

this moment
into being.

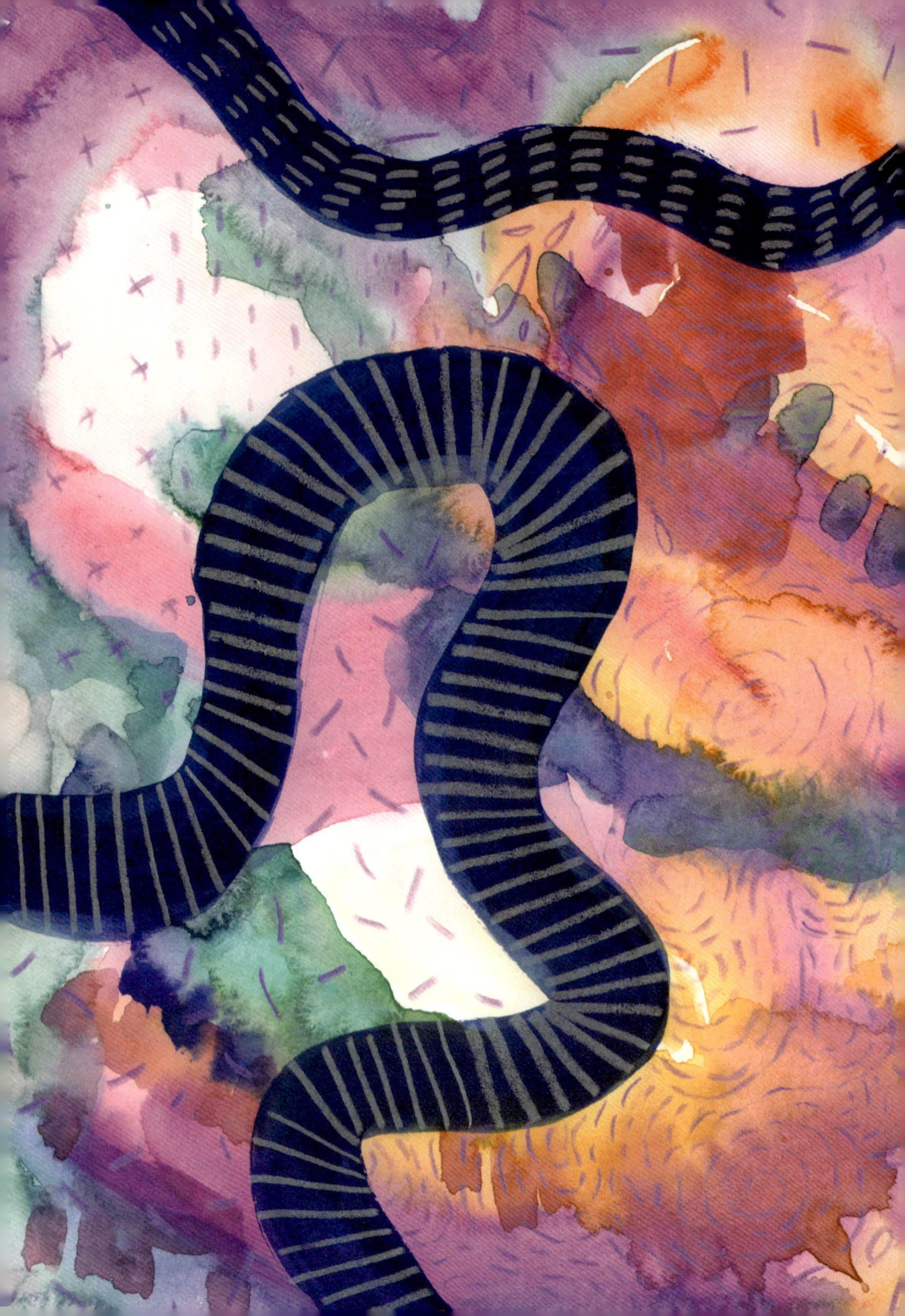

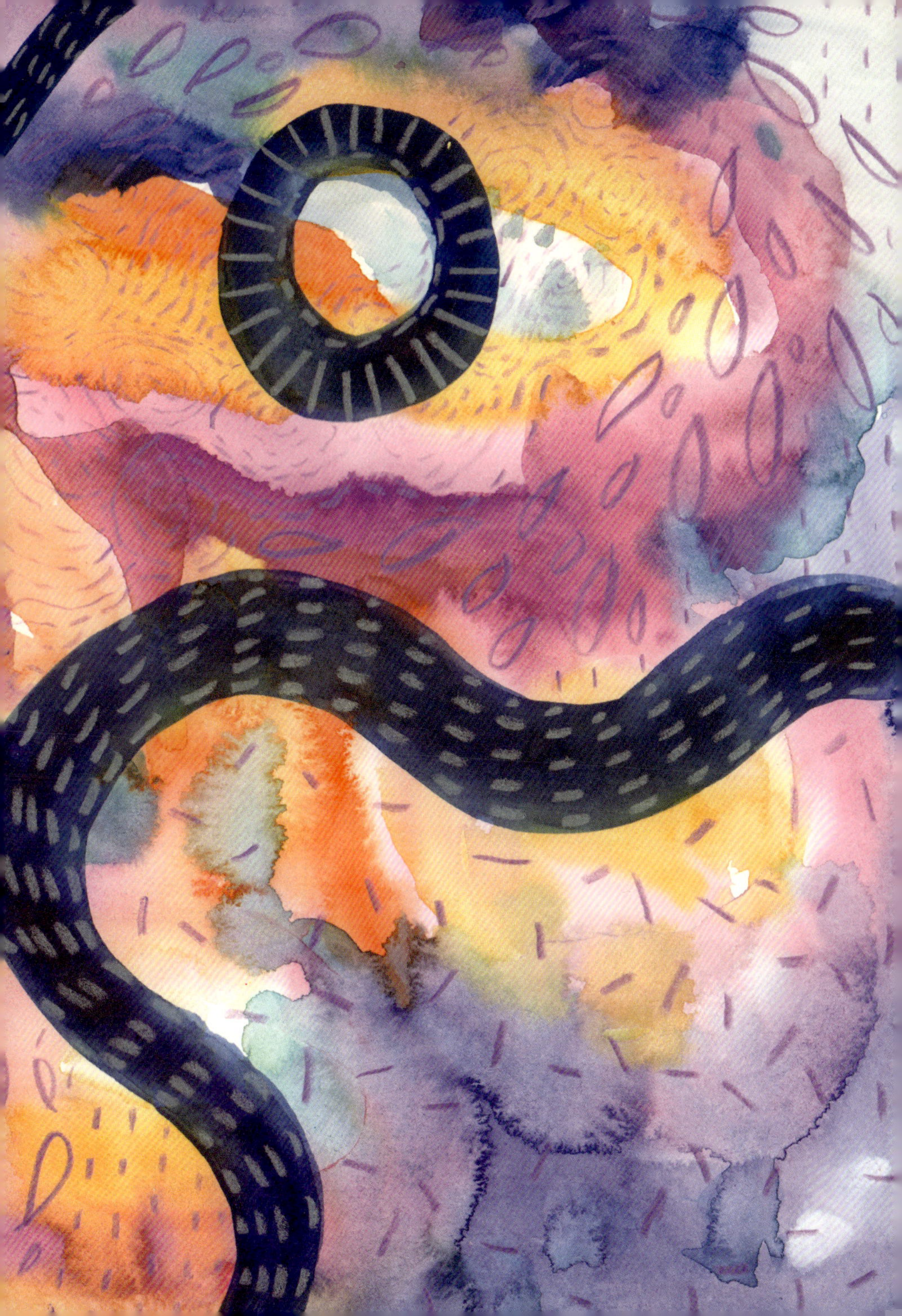

Sewing Hands

~ For Nan, and our sacred time spent
making my nephew and niece's first quilts

Your sewing hands
have fed fabric under foot
for more than double my lifetime

have held thread to teeth
for careful cutting

mosaiced square after square
in perfect formation
to orate a story
for intended
snugglee

measured bodies
for nighties
and PJ pants

knitted scarfs
every summer

delivered library bags
to kindergarteners
just in time for big school.

As I hold them
over tea

I pray that
I might inherit
some of their magic,

that I might learn
to feed
and cut
and warm,

that I could measure up

and create something,
to carry stories
with care,
just like
your sewing hands.

Garring | Possum Skin Cloak

~ For Aunty Loretta Parsley who helped me make my Cloak,
and my friends and family who gifted me my pelts for my 30th

We - call - upon - the - lessons - of - Aunties
who - learnt - from - theirs
        wake - sleeping - hands
        to - mend - and - make
                welcome - ants - who - devour - flesh
                and - carve - echidna - quill
                needles - and - roo - sinew
                - thread.
        Our - cloaks - grow
        older - with - us
        each - year - and - hold
        our - stories
        of - kin - and - land
        on - skin.
We - fuse - fingers
with - fur
ash - ochre - and - resin

Garring – cloak made from skins (Gundungurra)

Our - Ancestors - bless - each - stitch
of - preparation
each - stride - taken
to - be - on - this - path
of - rematriation,
every - second - invested
in - sewing - futures
late - into - the - night
where - calm - and - strength
are - cultivated
under - stars - and - moon - bright
and - salty
in - the - out - of - the - way - spaces
we - made
to - come - together
to - rematriate.

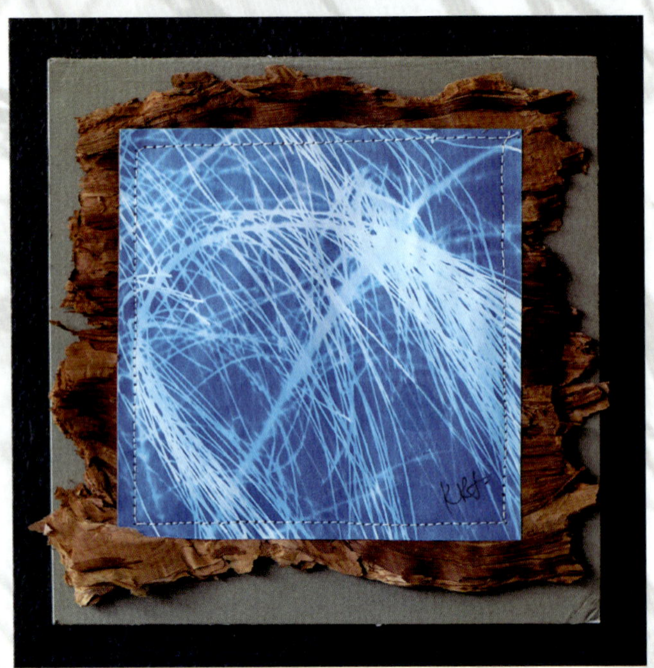

Bundjalung to Gadigal ~ A Love Poem

Carpet snake
city lights
map the land below

all brake-light-red
and headlight-yellow
It's been a beat since I've flown

and this —
my first time
coming Home
to you.

Spirit tree
to my mudji
nest, branch
and bower

understand they scoured
the sky and land
to shape
our interwoven ways
inseparable

trust how
the Old Ones
create

innate knowing
under every action

attention to detail
in each
stroke

unspoken wisdom
charting
all the ways

to land me
here

right here

with you.

mudji – friend

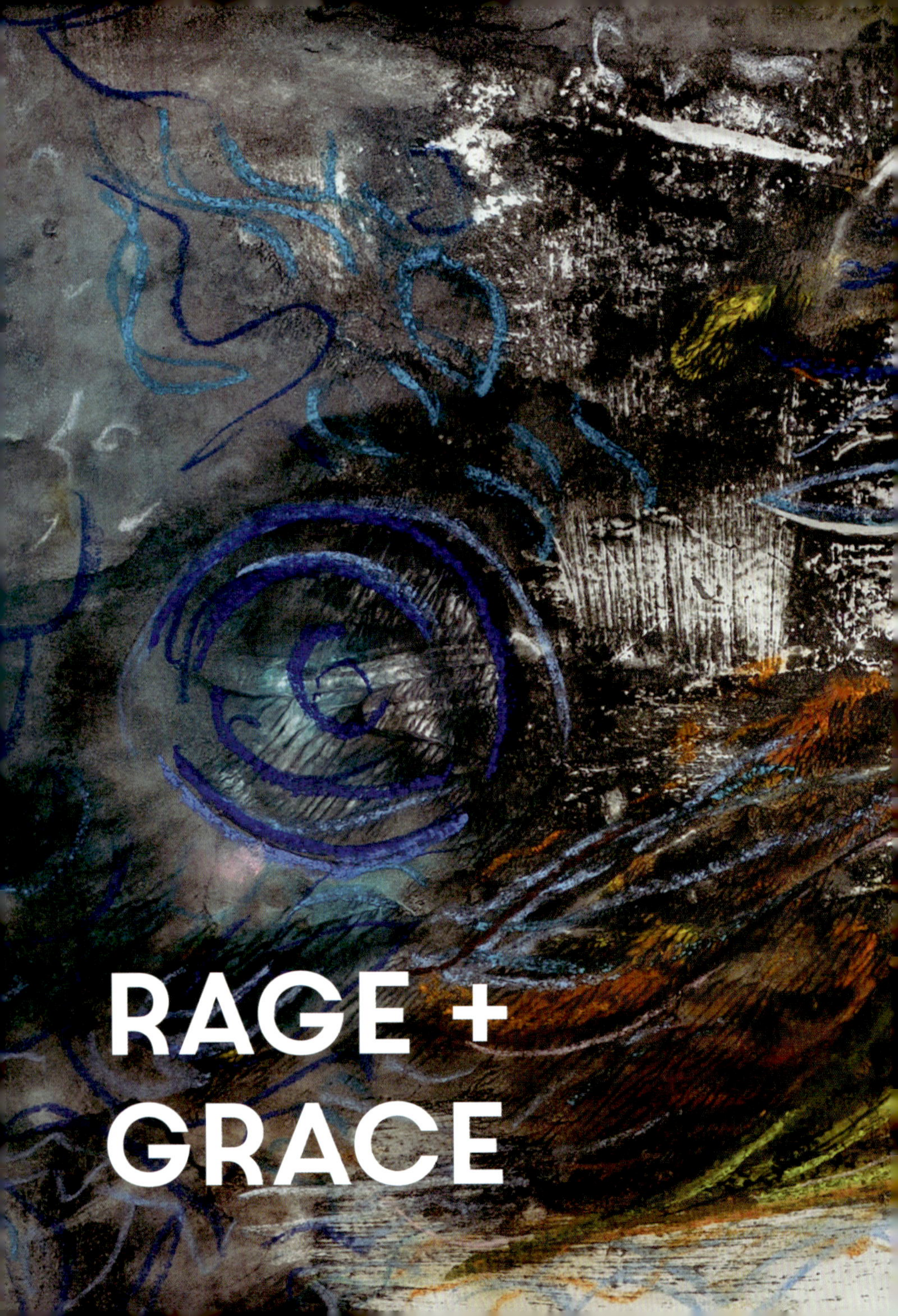
RAGE +
GRACE

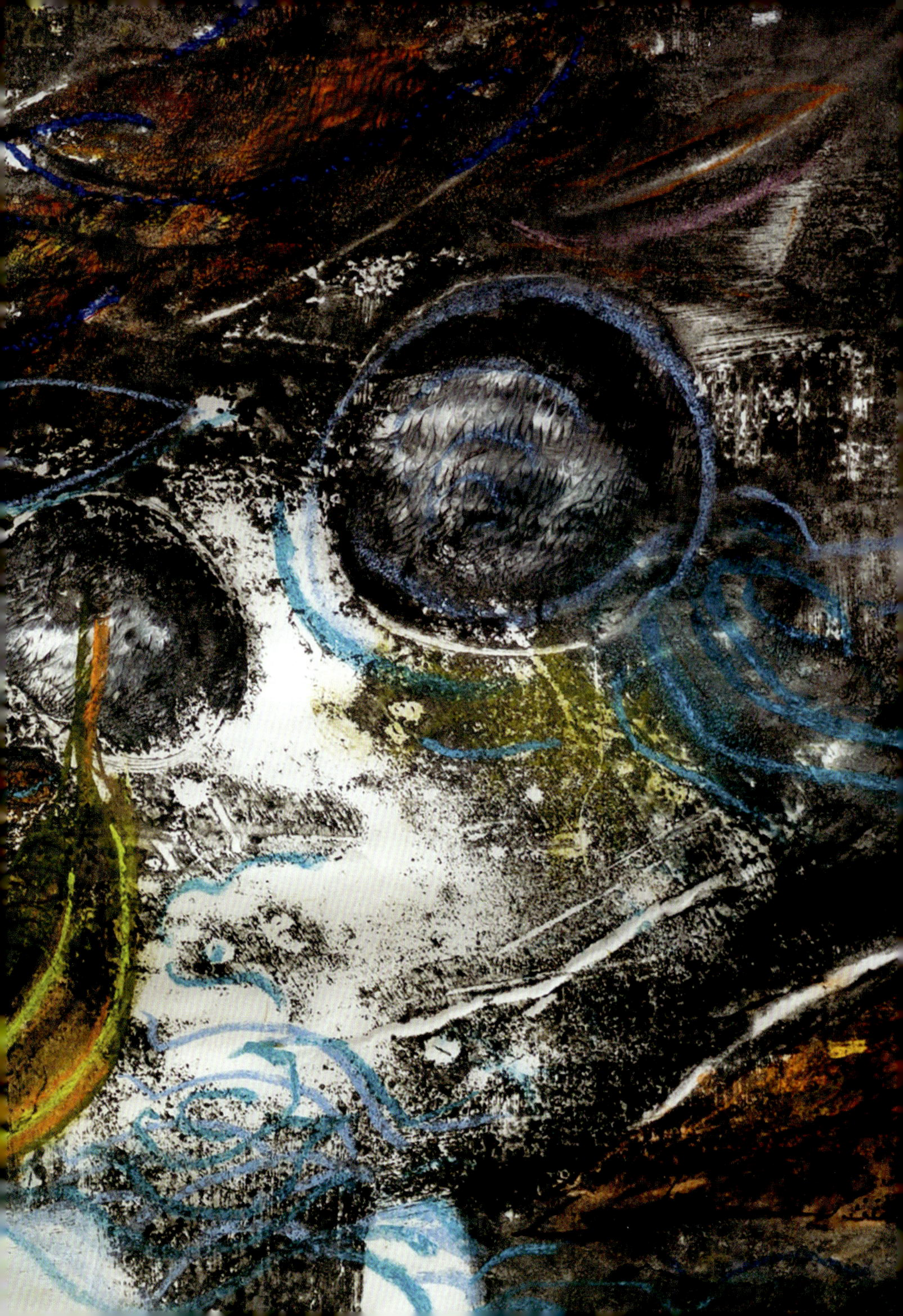

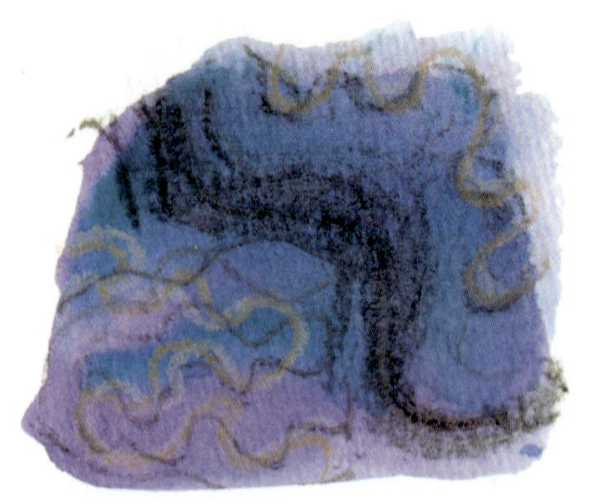

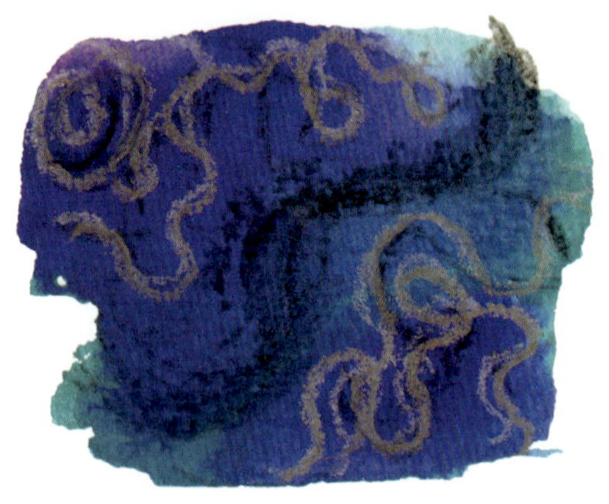

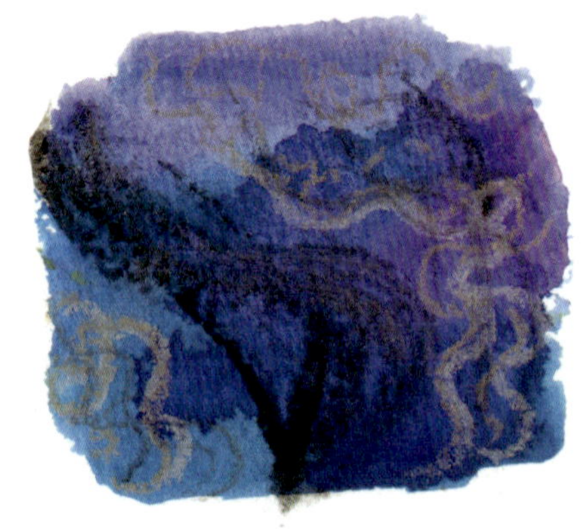

Black Cars

~ For our Grannies, with sincere gratitude for the Gundungurra language taught by Aunty Velma Mulcahy, Aunty Sharyn Halls and, through her, the work of Jim Barrett

Nga see the Burringiling-nyinang
stand by the doorframe
next to ashen bucket
filled with white soot

the dust
on maranga
and apron —
signs of the spells
smoothed on faces
to ward off black cars
they will not see you today

Nga sense the maarang bank
on phantom toes
like breadcrumbs —
guides to map you
to the places
that guudhaa were hidden

these remnants as offerings
to deter black cars
they will not find you today

Burringiling – the Gundungurra Ancestors/People (the far past times)
nyinang – our (possessive)
maranga – fingers
maarang – river
guudhaa – children

I see your outline
guwark over shoulder
before issuing card-table lessons,
a curriculum in gammuang pialla
for guudhaa underfoot.

This ritual of salt mil
over shoulders —

a spell
to impede black cars

they will not take you today

I witness your shadows
peel back the corners
of drapes
and numbul —
with midung mil open —
the door always ajar

these ancient omens,
to eradicate black cars

you are safe

I gamiri your presence
in careful mothers,

hear your voice
in gunyunggalung pialla sons —

gummuang pialla – Mother talk
mil – eye
numbul – sleep
midung – one
gunyunggalung – the Dreaming

your Burringiling lives
in guudhaa
that will march
against a Government
that once issued
the collection of guudhaa
in black cars

always one step ahead

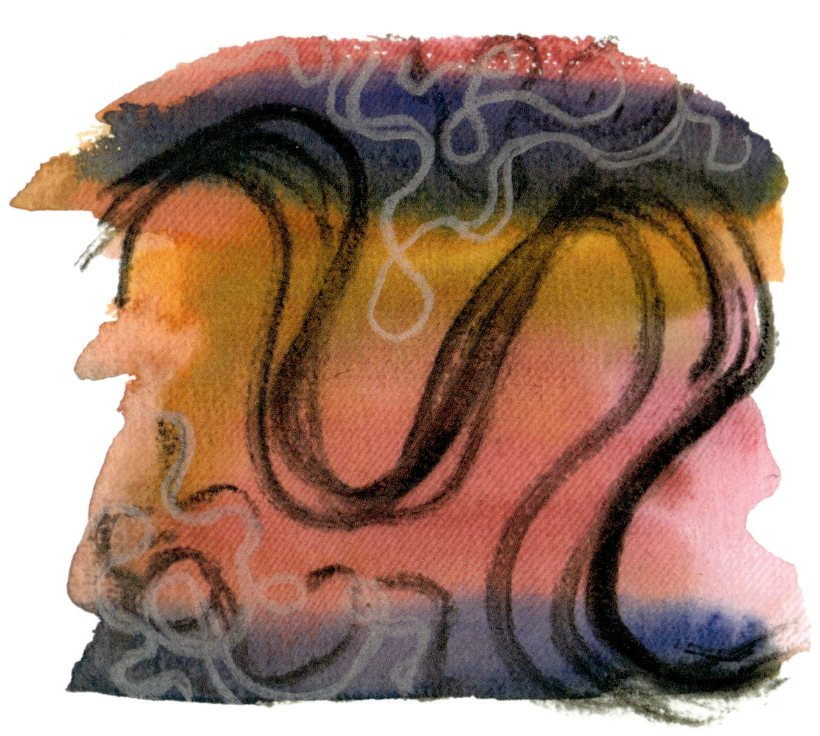

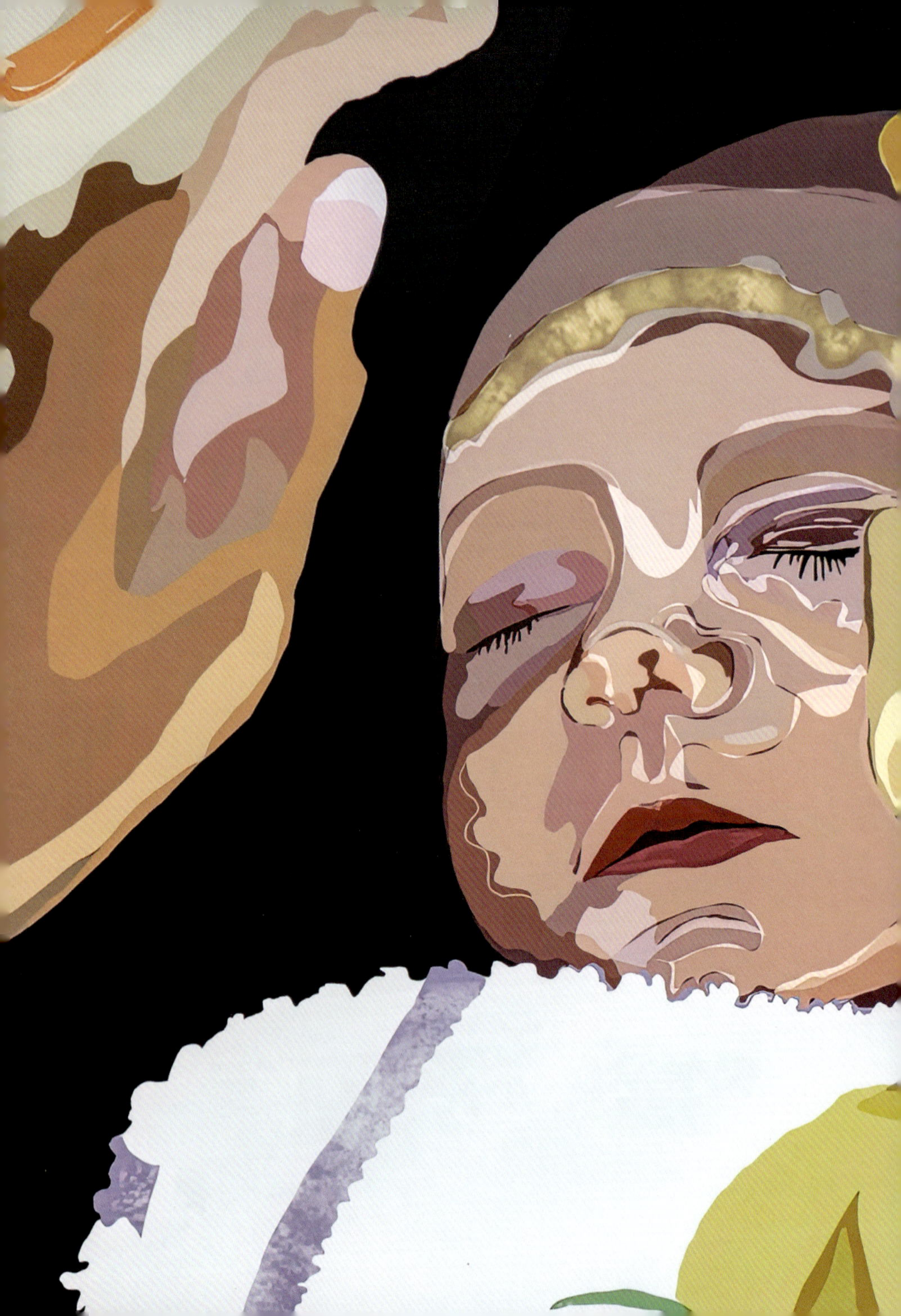

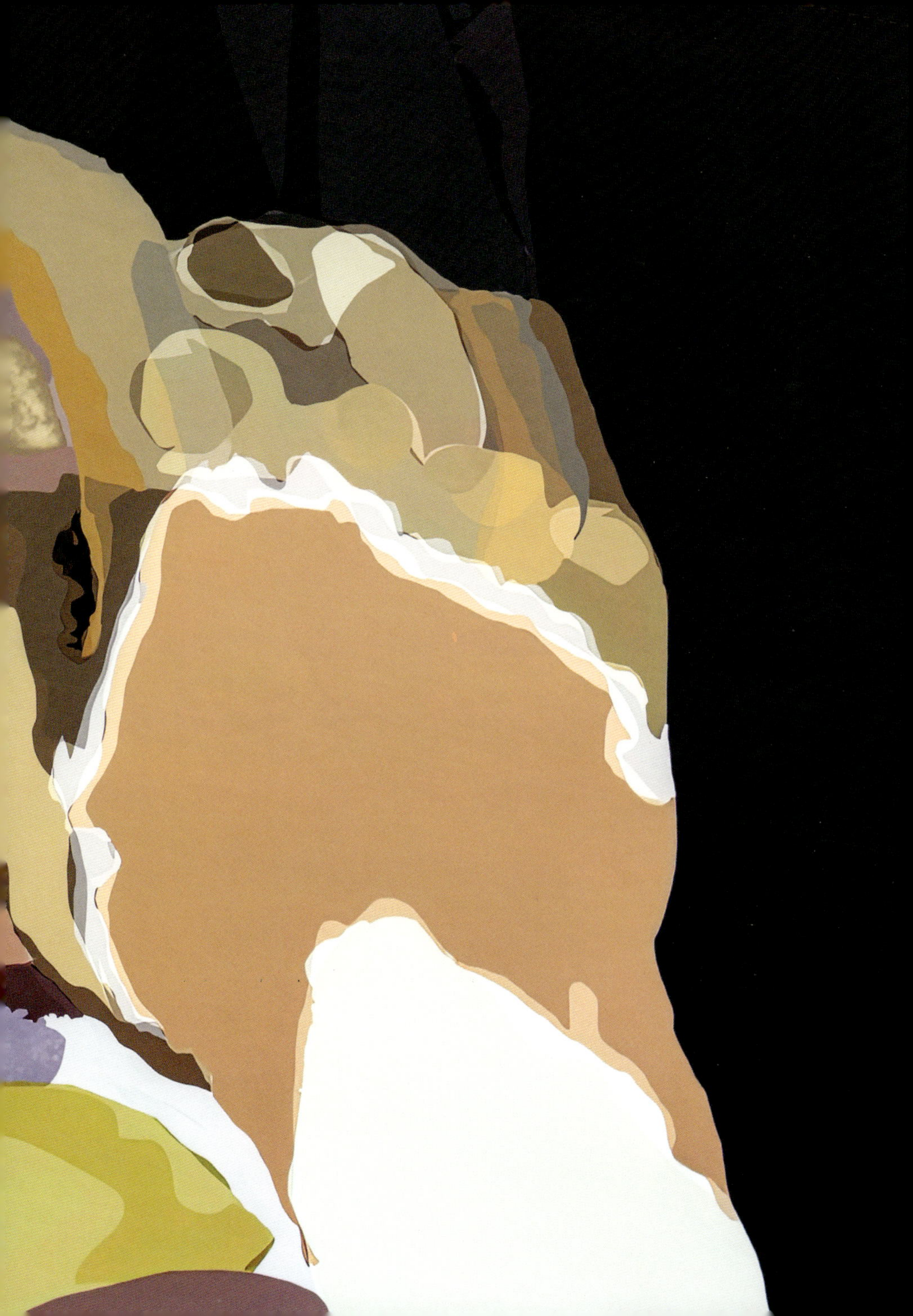

Yabun

~ For those who dance. With sincere gratitude for the Gundungurra language taught by Aunty Velma Mulcahy, Aunty Sharyn Halls and, through her, the work of Jim Barrett

I

Aunty Lou
rounds Mum's face
with a riverside blessing

smoothing healing
in place of shame

she paints us in gubity
with markings different
to guudhaa.

This is their first Yabun

and though
we are of age
and have been for a time

this is our first too.

Gundungurra Language
gubity – white ochre
guudhaa – children
Yabun – Corroboree

II

We follow
the Aunties
through dyumbak

teach the young ones how to breathe
and bathe off
bad spirit

watch the Men
teach the boys the same

listen to the Elders
who are 'too old' to tangara

as they welcome us
and show us
why we are here

to honour Gummuang Daore
to carry the rain

back to chapped lips
creeks, cheeks
and rivers.

dyumbak – smoke
tangara – dance
Gummuang Daore – Mother Earth

III

It's been 159 years

since our feet have been
burnt, sealed and healed
by black earth

since hands
have clapped
dyindyii and raw

our voices coarse
with yanggang
up the spirit of Country
under Ngaabuung Bunyal

today,
our tangara
will shake the dry

and we will swell
and sway with Burringiling

dyindyii – red
yanggang – song
Ngaabuung Bunyal – Grandfather Sun
Burringiling – the Gundungurra Ancestors

welcoming abundance
home
to this land

proudly united
we stand and wait
for Aunt to start.

She raises her hands
reminding us

that our Old People
know the way

our Old People
know the way.

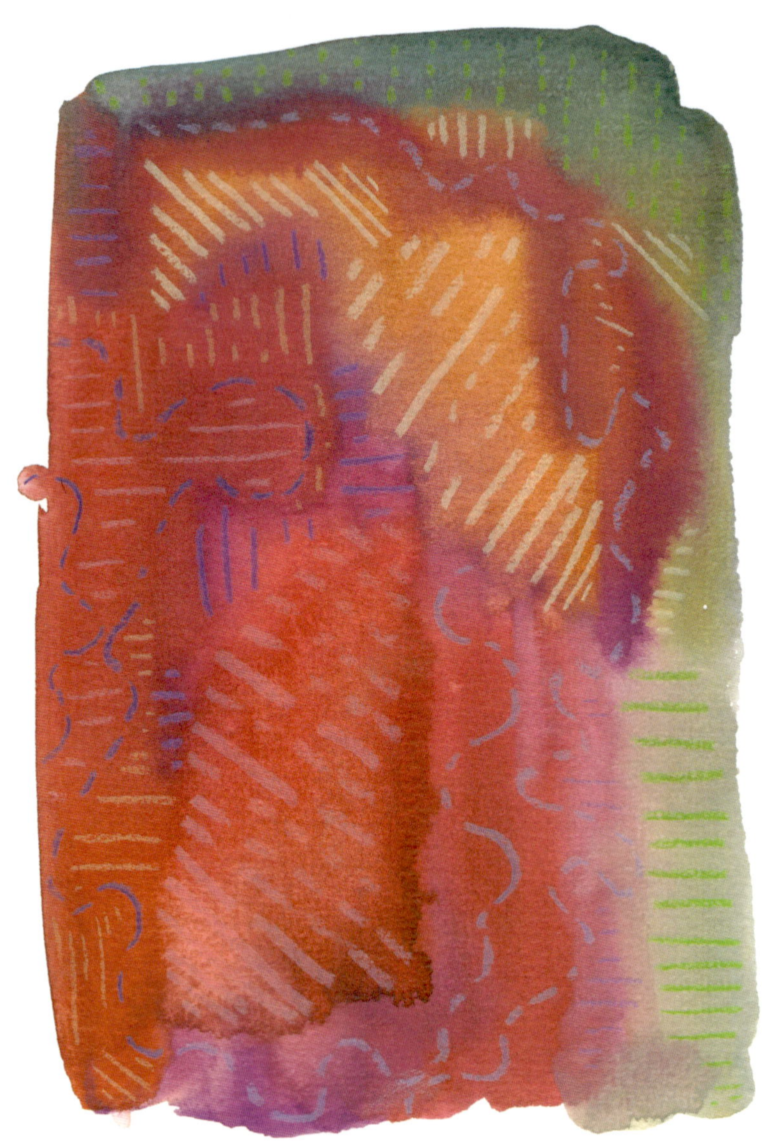

#realtalk

The Marketing Man says
‘there was no slavery in Australia’

omitting

South Sea Islander families
falsely recruited, lured or forced
onto boats
who laboured far from home
in sugarcane plantations
on land named after
the coloniser’s Queen

‘there was no slavery in Australia’

forgetting

Our saltwater Mothers
who dove with lung capacity greater
(for the babies inside them)
and were left in the water
if they didn’t return
a pearl

‘there was no slavery in Australia’

ignoring

Former Australian Prime Minister Scott Morrison claimed there was ‘no slavery in Australia’ during an interview with 2GB radio, 2020.

Our Fathers
whose remuneration for unpaid labour
is still being pursued
who signed away their home | family | culture
with exemption certificate
to make a life the white way
and were still denied
human rights

'there was no slavery in Australia'

disregarding

Our Uncles
who fought side by side
under union jack
in global combat
only to return to
Assimilation, the Stolen Generations
and no right to vote.

'there was no slavery in Australia'

neglecting

Our Sisters held as
domestic servants
Our Brothers working
the longest days
on cattle stations
both paid a fraction
of the wage
of their caucasian mates
in a time where work health and safety didn't exist

and the mistreatment
of our people was commonplace —
legally endorsed
in the constitution

The Marketing Man
could call for referendum now,
vote to have more of Our People in power
support land back
compensate our families for past harms
hand the mic over
to us

instead he wastes airtime with
acoustic lies like
'there was no slavery in Australia'.

The System

ACAB but this one smiles at me
as I enter the bottle shop

he checks my ID
sees I'm an out-of-towner
waves me on —
no worries
for Kooris.

As I leave
with ciders
underarm

Uncle is turned away —
wrong postcode, see

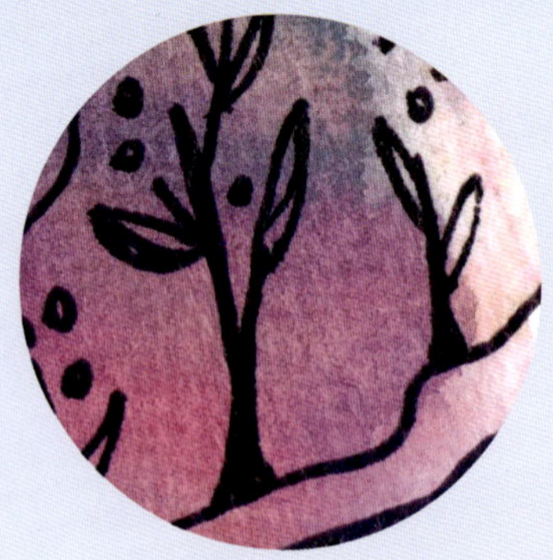

no relief from the
addiction created
by white man's poison
and greed

no understanding
for his habit
or the inherited hurt it may ease

just a wave off

move along mate

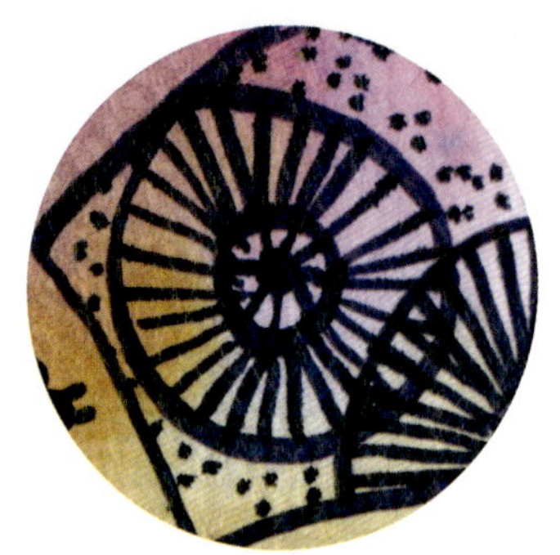

our eyes meet for a beat
with the guilt and grief of existing
in this violent settler-colonial state

as someone of Country
and someone off Country.

We part ways
at the sounds of sirens.

In the carpark a ten year old child is taken away
in a paddy wagon

their mother screams in lingo
with occasional translation
for officers

he's just a kid
let my baby go

I said

Let *My* *Baby* *Go!*

on the way back to camp
I pull over

pour all
the cider
out

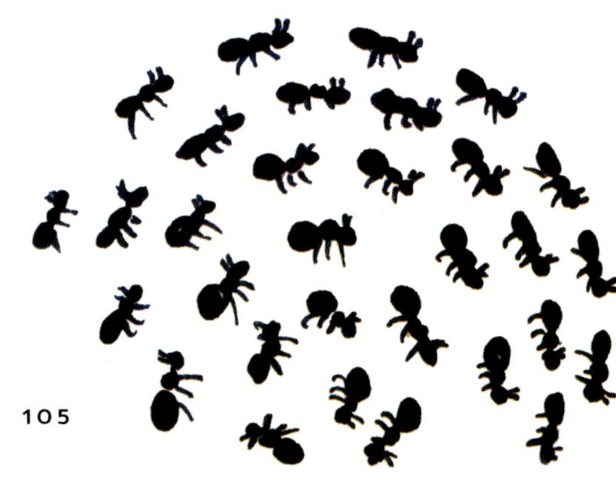

crush the cans and let
a potion of heavy tears and booze
pool and soak
in dry-season soil

spoilt ants
leave roadkill remains
with an eagle across the way

they gather at the sticky red billabong
savouring the offering

their swaying bodies signalling —
none of us
are safe
in this system.

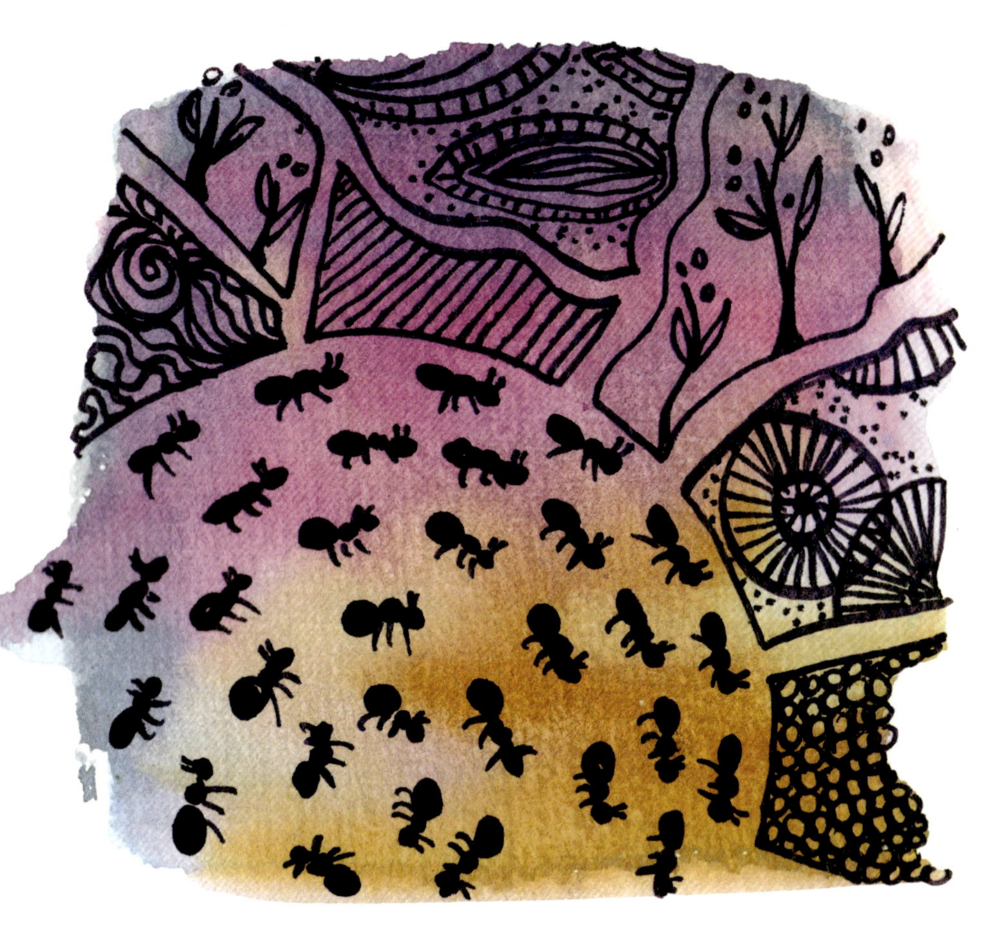

Vinegar and Bicarb

She dusts
she mops
she folds
before the dawn
dressed in white
she stands tall
shoulders down
she keeps
our house
our home
clean.

She bakes
she roasts
she steams
makes the place gleam
some more
in case they come
with papers
and combs —
with teeth fine
for finding fault
just as they did before
when she was small.

She polishes
she sweeps
she presses
school dresses
like those they
wore in the homes
and on the mish —

a uniform
looking swish
with all of us
the same —
a wash of white
for clothing
and skin
and tongues
and brain —
for pain
now supposed to be gone
like the dust —
that will return.
This is why she cleans.

Gubinge

~ For Aunty Pat

Kate takes us to Nyul Nyul

says we gotta go visiting

Aunt shows us her block

I marvel at
land agreements
unlike ours at home

at ochre cliffs
who melt into aqua

brahminy kites above
blue bones below

Aunt walks us through her gubinge

talks about harvest
handed down over millennia

flashes videos
of wet season delivery
as west coast sun ripens
and falls

two tonnes of fruit
off to Naarm
for processing

| engine off | towed by truck | no snorkel on the ute | trailer
bobbing | red mud splashing and staining | her husband drives
imprinted road | he's done this before | window down
wipers broken | Rex the dog sits up |

I wonder if the company pays well
if Aunt and the other local growers
get a proper cut of the profit
for the monsoon lengths they go to

I hope they do

family up here know that
bush medicine
could heal
us all

so they share
generously
like
their
gubinge
trees.

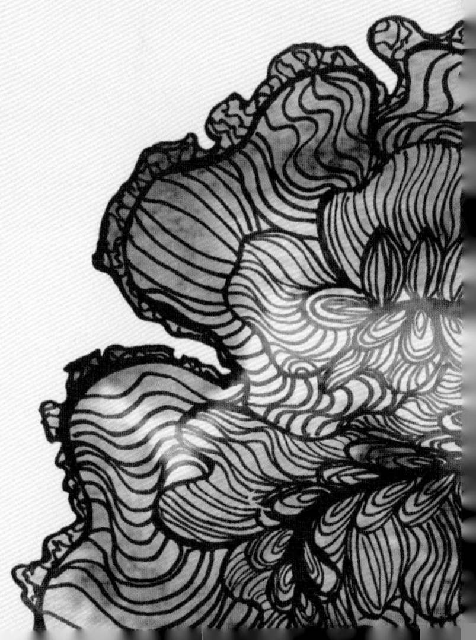

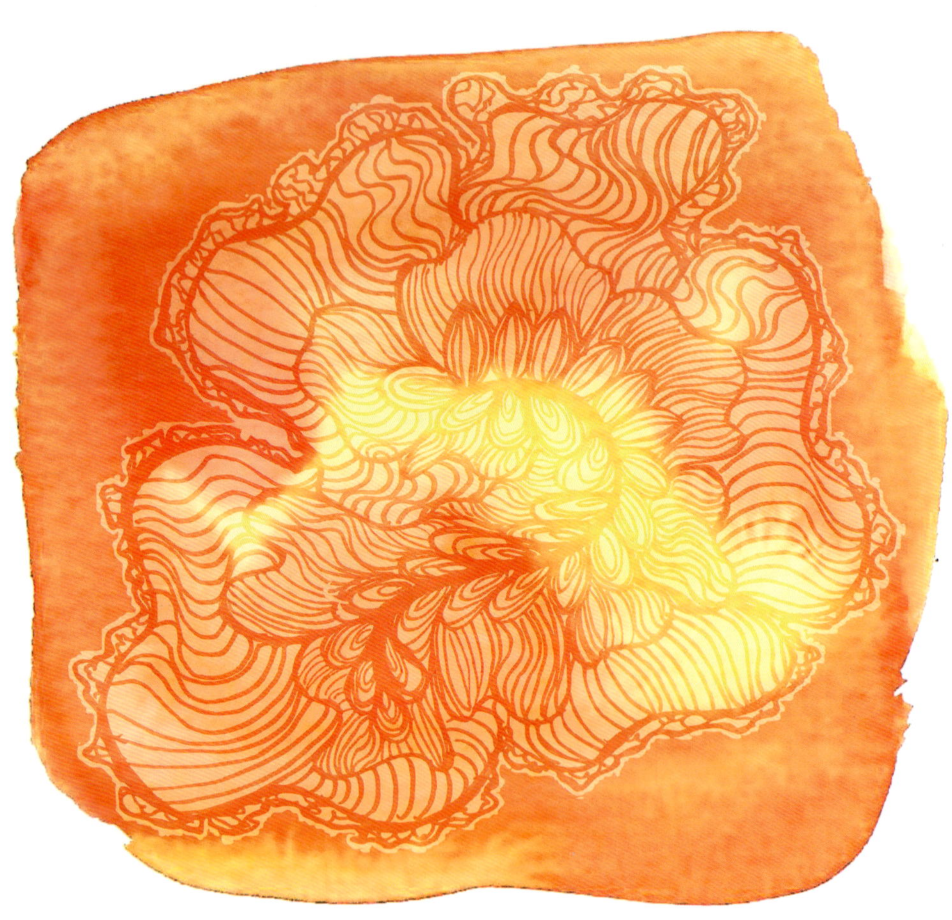

W/e/l/c/o/m/e

She spelled out welcome in feathers
as we crossed into Brayakaulung

introduced us to Sky,
Land and River

who knew Nan
and all my Kin

I watched Kite ascend again,
the twitching tips of her
shifting in intuitive adjustment

through wind lifting wings
I heard them ask
'how's it feel to be home, Bub?'

(to have found us despite
grand displacement
and erasure?)

I studied the bird close then,
found comfort in her trust
in the currents
watched her braiding
corroboree belts from clouds

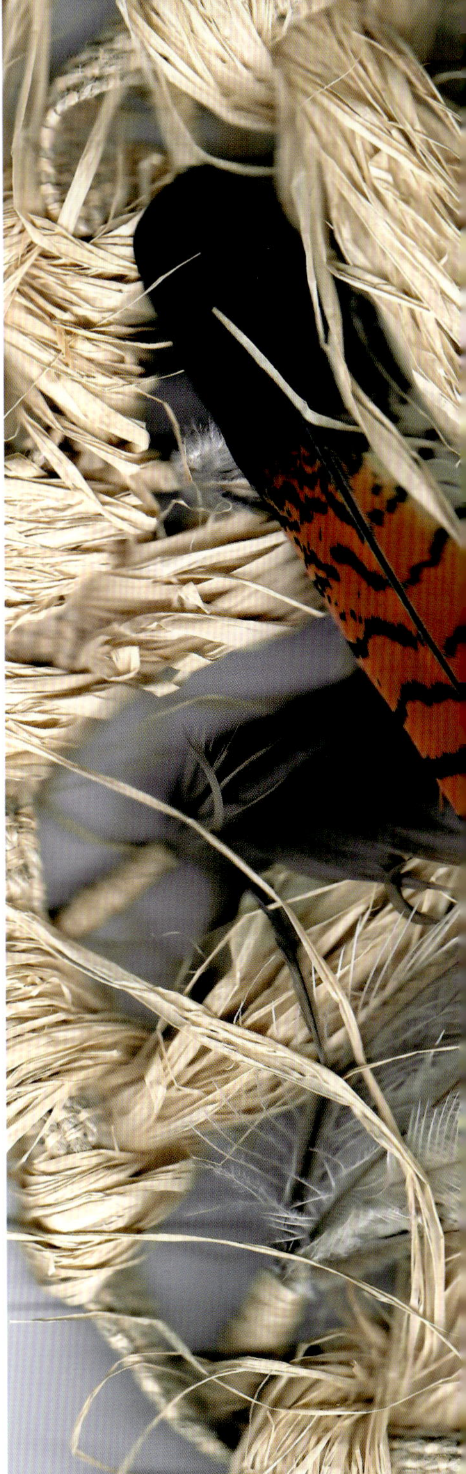

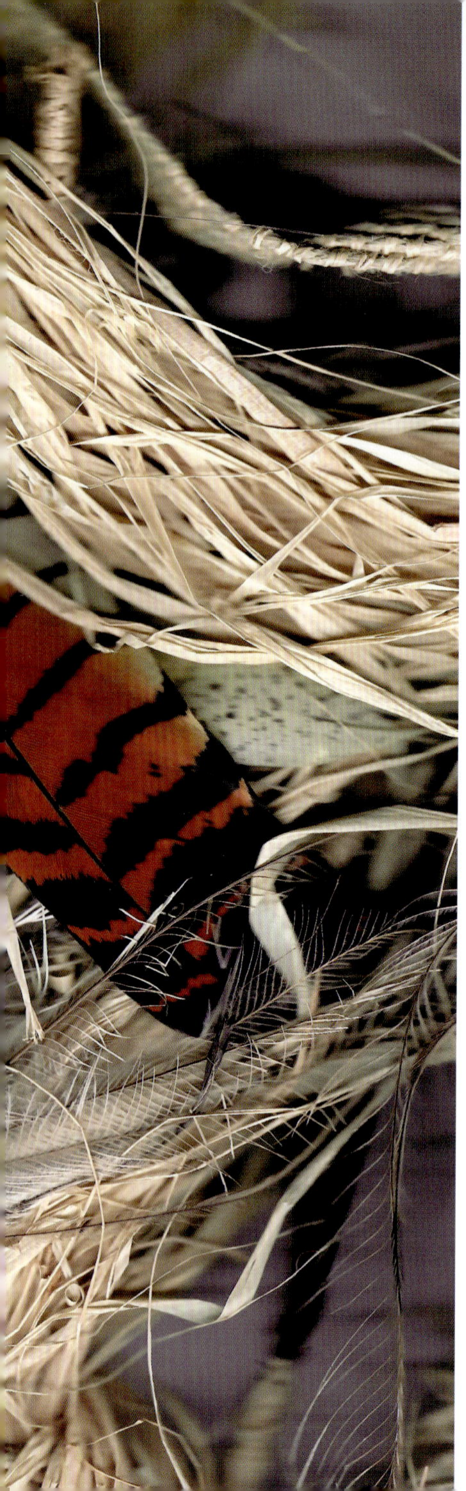

and nodded

it's like weaving

eyes closed
hands soft
wrapping
pulling

like leaning into the knowing
just as Mum taught me
and Nanny Hoskins taught her

like shaping
a belt to adorn hips
to sway and stomp and step my way
all the way back south
to the land of Lakes and Sea

where my feet follow
the rhythm of thousands of years
of powerful dancers.

Like coming home.

And with that
Kite was gone.

Aunty time

~ For Aunty Pippy and Sam

When my sister comes home on the full moon
we howl at her
teaching our nephew new tricks
on the balcony
under swinging mountain ash and gums
who raised us too.

He is learning
to talk but doesn't have a word
for this yet

for our
wily time marking

for familial noise making with
belly breath billows
in cold Gundungurra air

he laughs at us as if one of the Old People,
as if remembering this lesson
from a time before

aroooooooooooooooooooooooo

we empty our lungs and fill
still suburban night with
the first words
the dingo spoke

aroooooooooooooooooooooooo

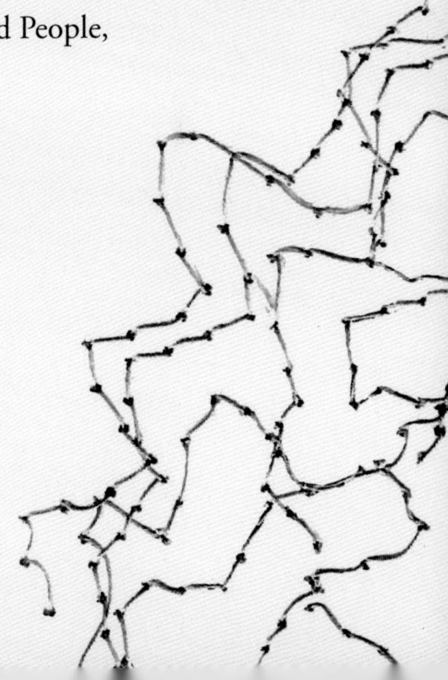

I point him to that songline there
the one who holds
this animal's story

arooooooooooooooooooooooo

he can't walk it
and doesn't have the name
for the escarpment yet

but we don't need those
for him to know
that he belongs here

that this is his story,
and his song
was written in sinew long before
he came along

that the ridge-line
moulded his very spine

and he is one
and the same —
with Country

that we move in unison
with Mother's time

with the night

with the light
of the moon

soft on smiling cheeks
as we

arooooooooooooooooooooooo

and renew the trust

that all is as it should be.

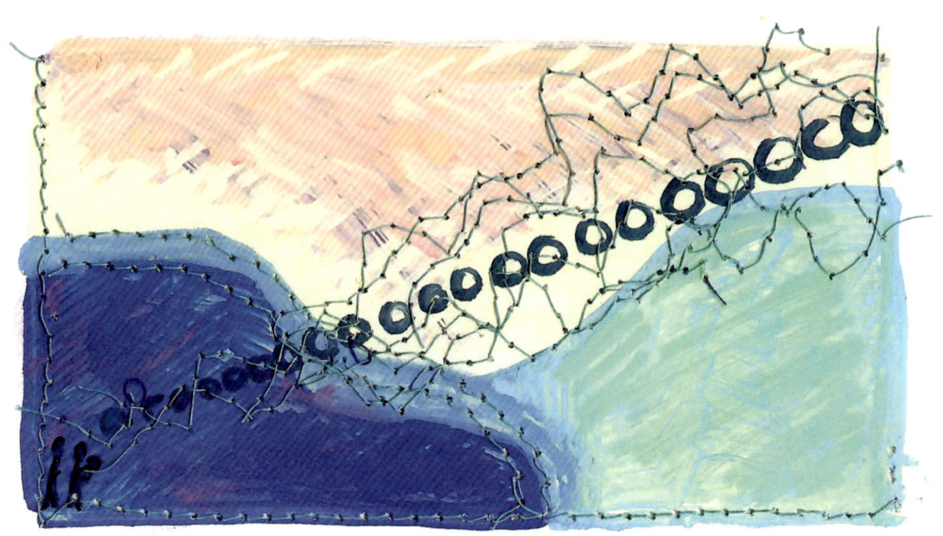

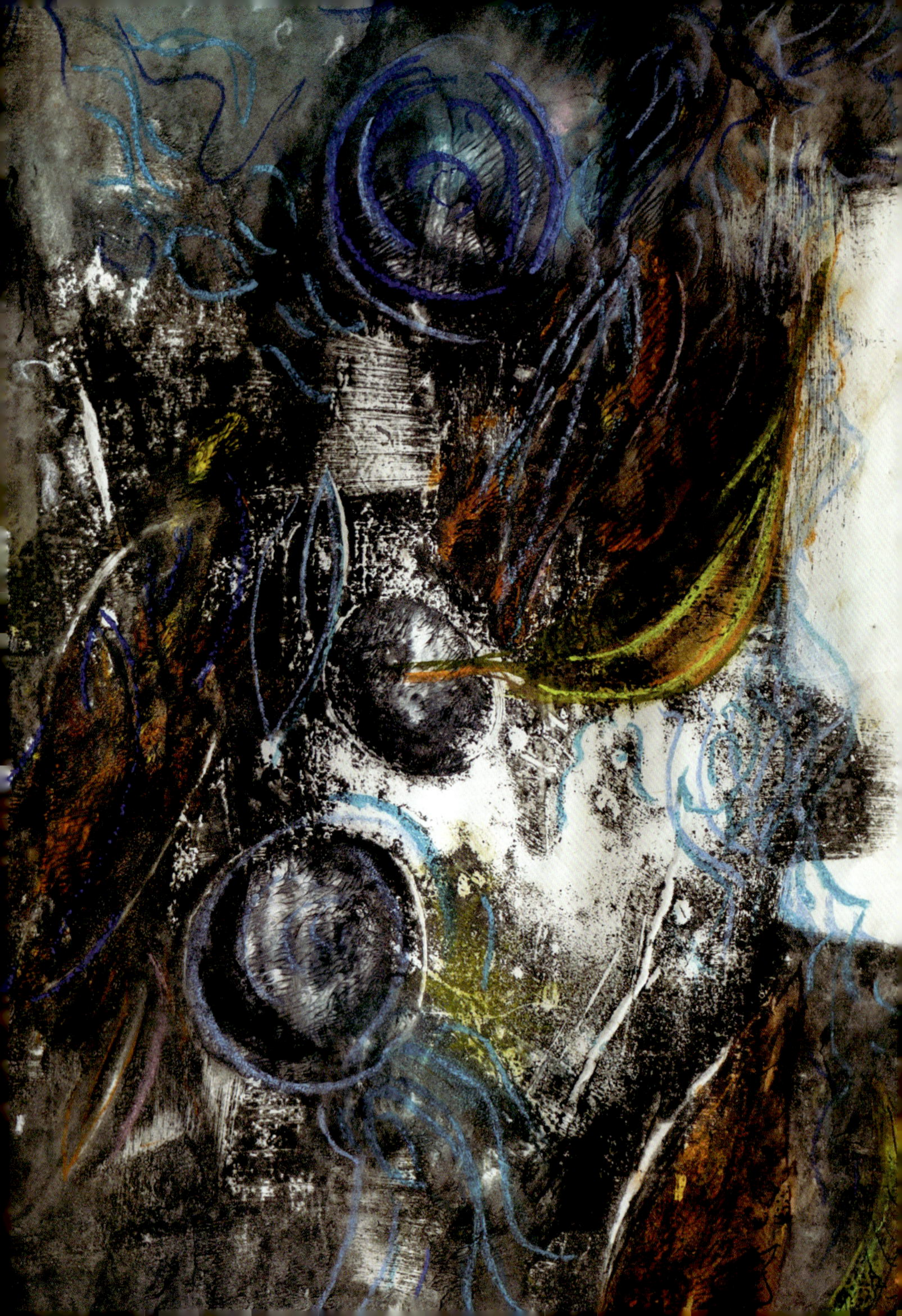

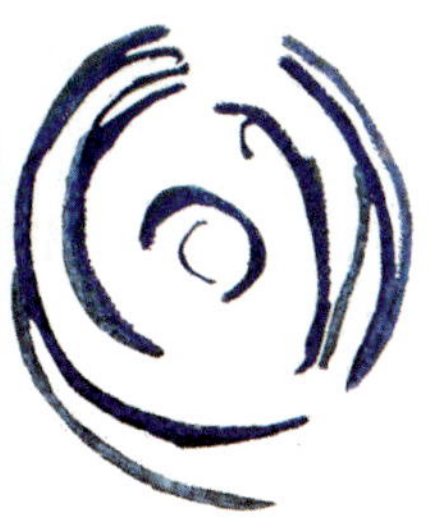

21st Century Custodians

After seeing the status
I call Aunt in my lunch break,
squeeze culture
into conversations
between emails

she calls me *Bub*
like always —
warmth like sap
flowing from her.

Today though,
she's tired —
sick of the careless
people in power
desecrating the land

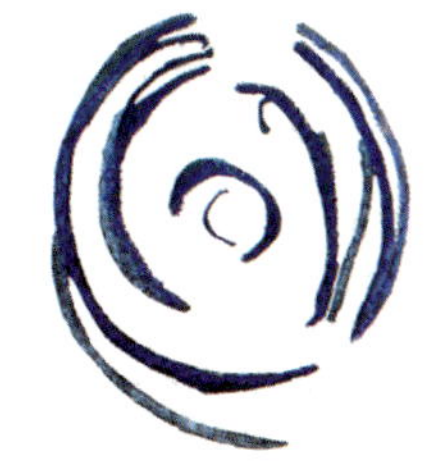

destroying sacred sites
with agendas

exhausted from fighting
with the passed buck
that bounces between
colonial disseminators.

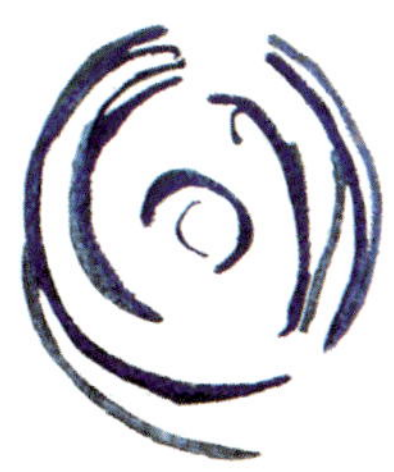

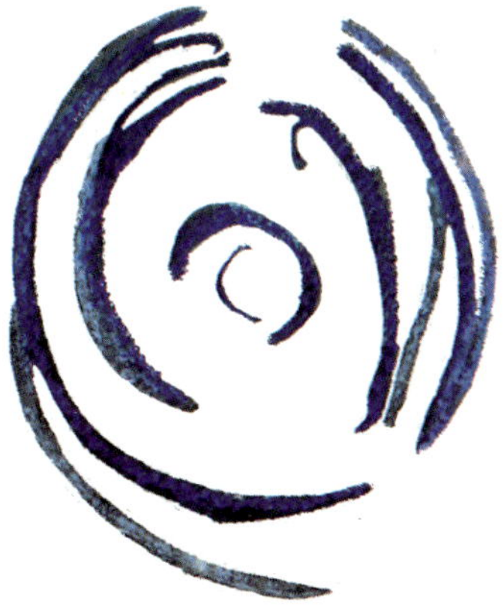

Today, her hands wear ashy marks
from tying white ribbons
on bushfire-charred Scar Trees —
a peace symbol
she hopes will stop
their sacred bodies
from being cut down
and forgotten
by authorities.

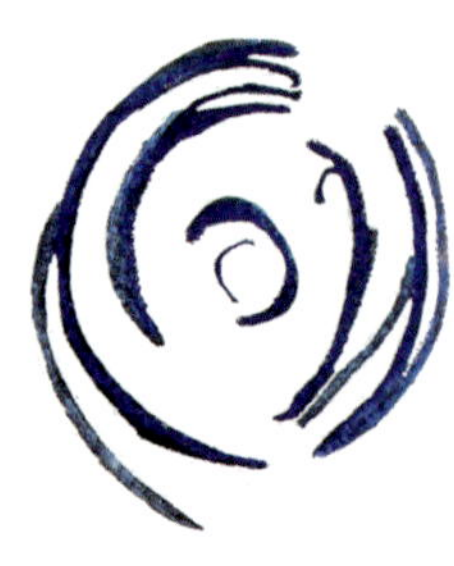

My hands are
stamped in bla(c)k
office ink
I open my fist and scan the spared
creases,
pick up the call to home —
and penning a note of absence.

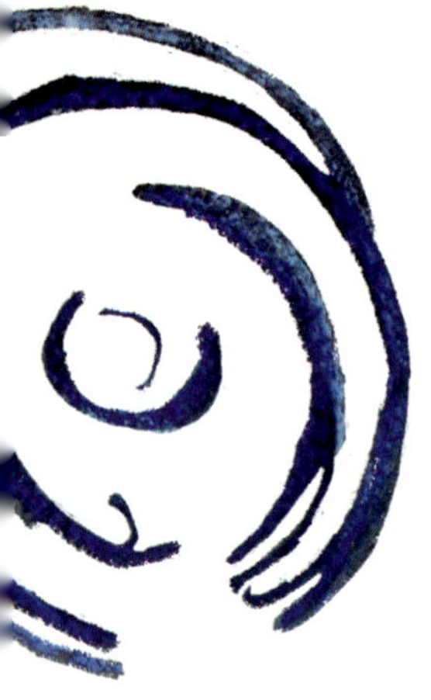

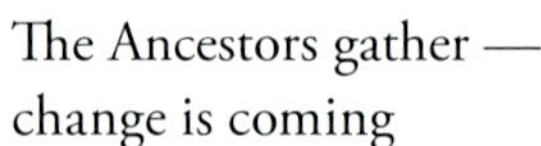

The Ancestors gather —
change is coming

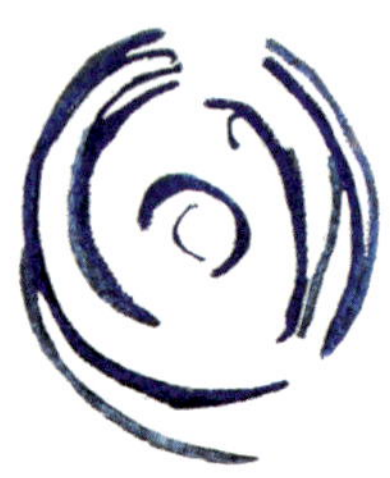

and office work can wait.

Community Possum Skin Cloak

~ With thanks to Aunty Loretta Parsley, Nicole Smede, Jo, Tamryn and the Oranges and Sardines Foundation and Bundanon Trust for supporting Aunt and I to teach a community possum skin cloak-making project on Banggali. And to all of the women who made this week so magical, thank you

monoprinted ferns
bakers dozen emerald bower birds
wattle marbled on Banggali
like creamed honey

sore thumb
cherry blossom
and fire weed
beneath shea-oak and gum

a meditation begun
with singing-bowl bees

the blue wren
fluffs feathers
and cleans beak
of insect crumbs

currawong slinks between
spotted and fig-strangled trees

egret
skips the stones
of her belly
on river skin

Banggali – Gumea Dharawal name for Shoalhaven River as taught to me by Jacob Morris.

within, mara
rejoice for the warmth of this day

noting the skies
and with them, seasons
always change

rays of sun
sling sticky silver linings
on clouds in celebration,
they knead the path
from mountains to sea
where
Country
Ancestors
and seven generations

are proud
of the sewing
we've done.

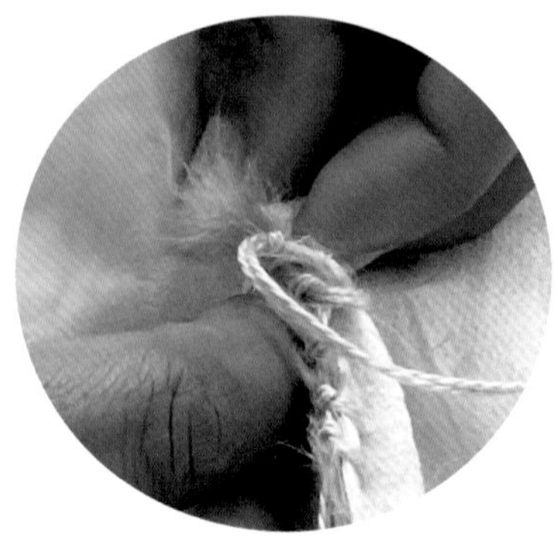

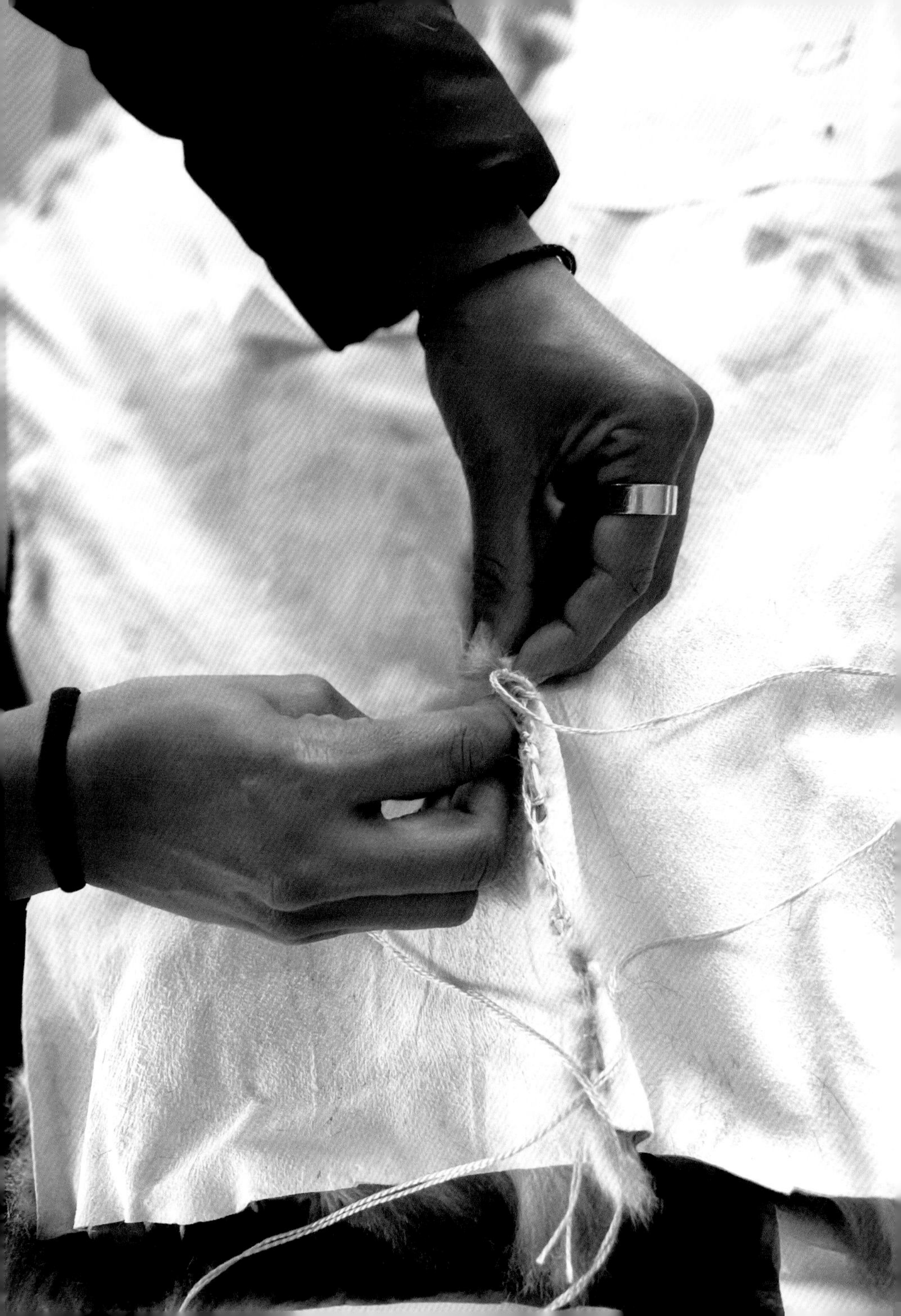

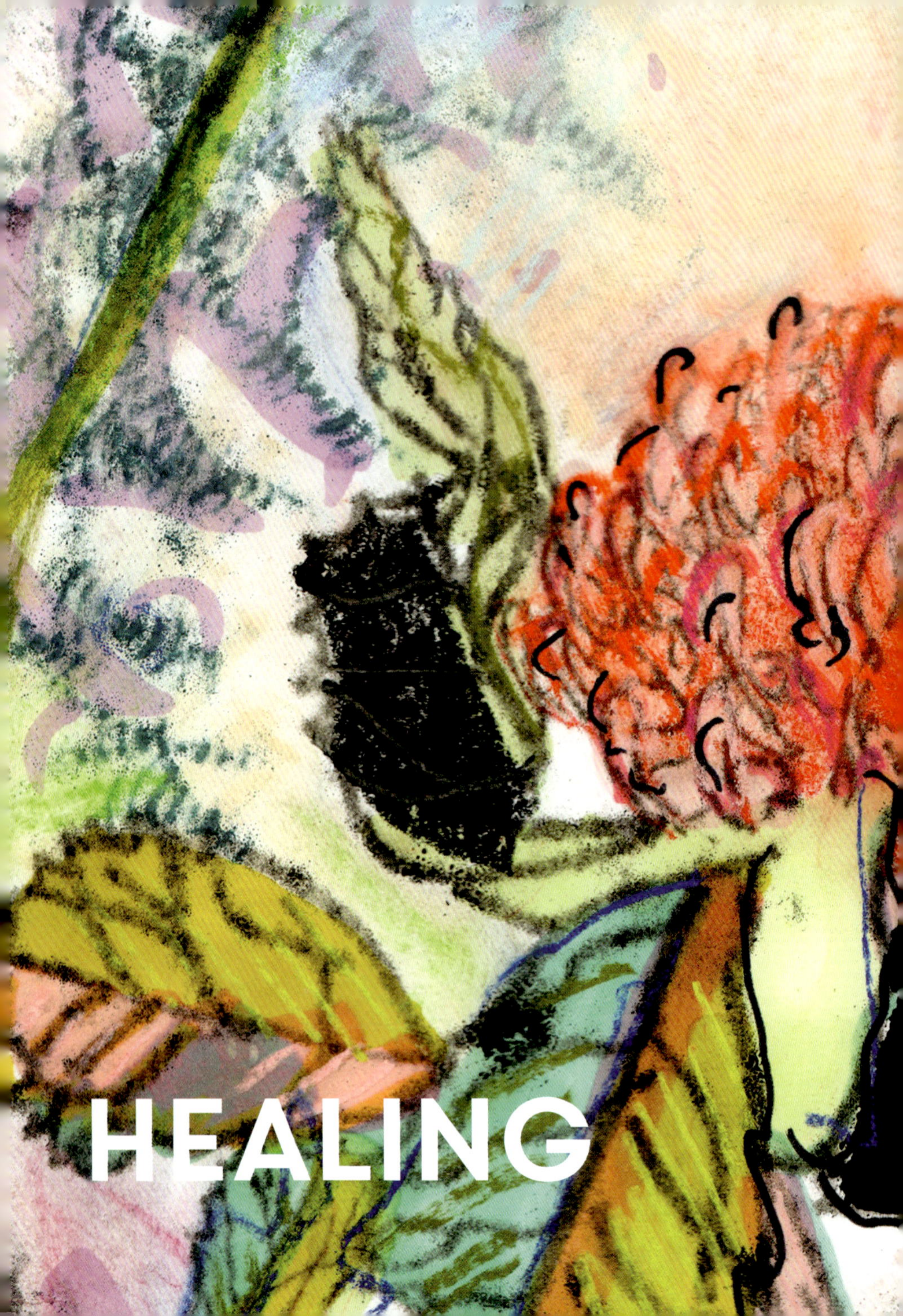
HEALING

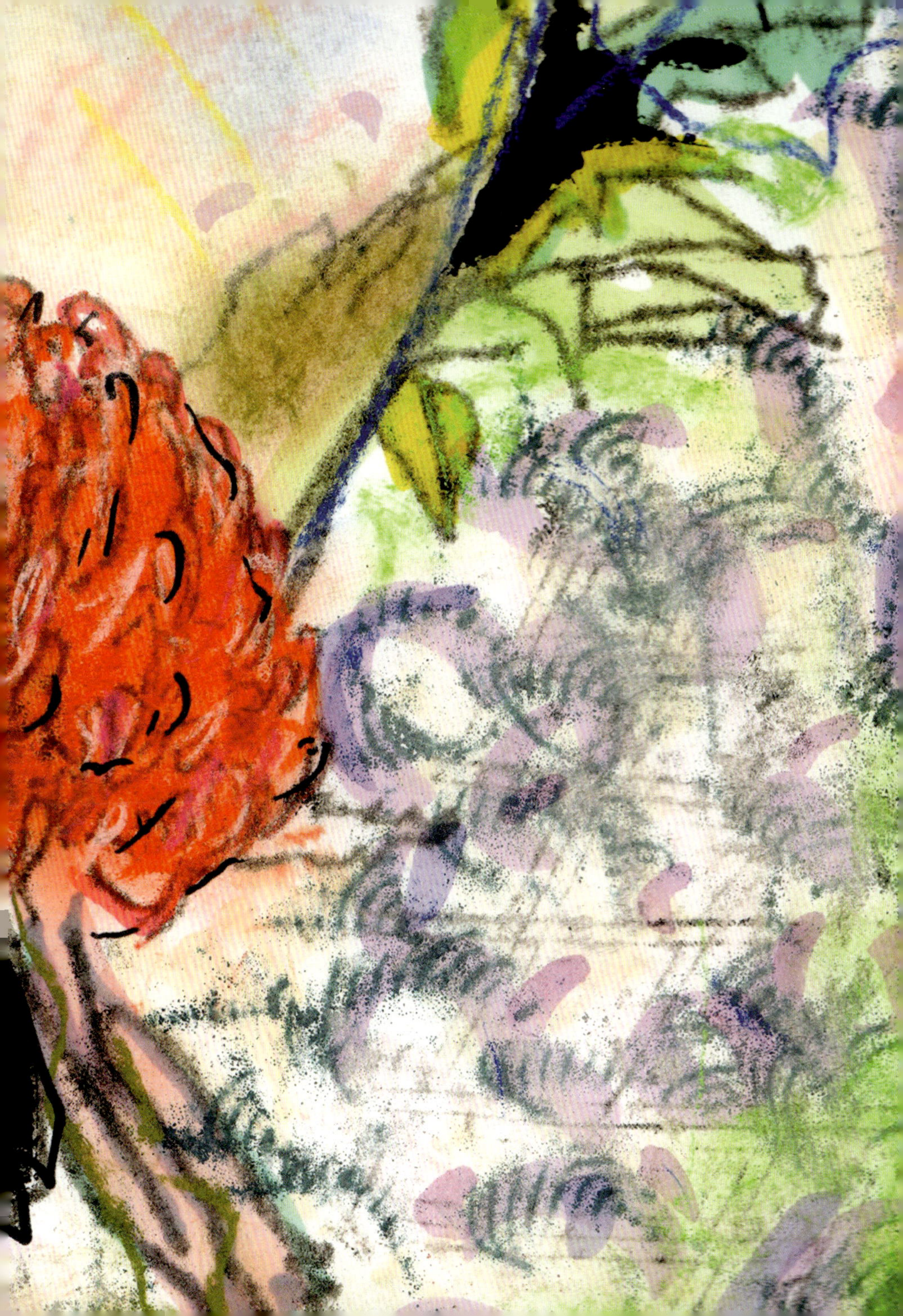

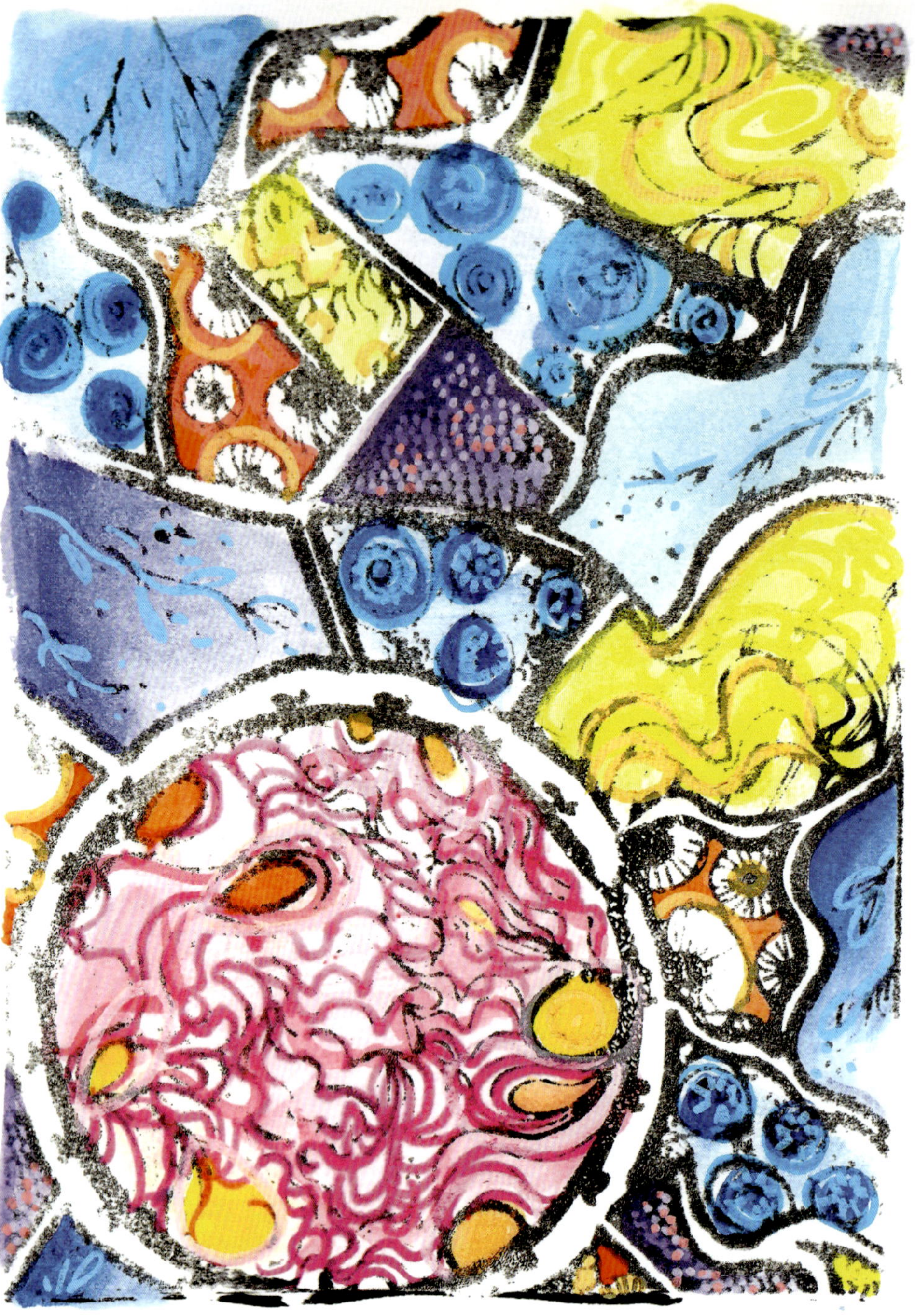

You Will Never Cry Alone

~ With love, for those who grieve

Our lashes have been salted in synergy

our lips quiver in synchronicity

there is simplicity
in breaking here —
and letting go.

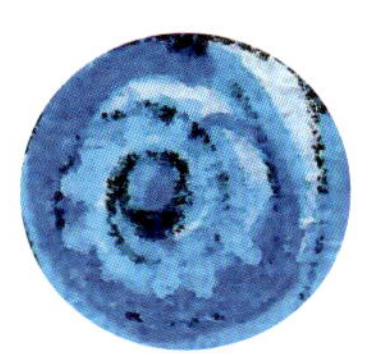

This shoulder was carved
for your cheek

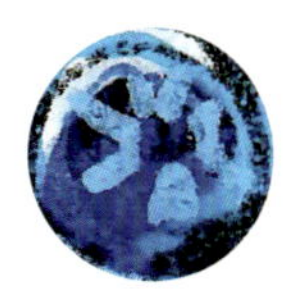

shattered with
aching grief

and this hand was made
to stroke it
back to calm,

these fingers —
to dance in your palms

and to honour
all that is physical
while it lasts.

As we sit by the water
we pause to remember

the ones we love,
who have passed.

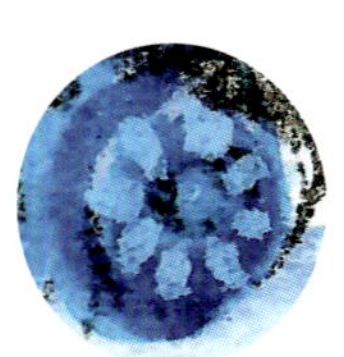

Eucalyptus Euphemism

When the diagnosis lands

she buys me flowers

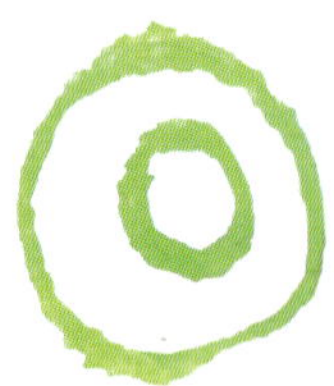

a softening offer
of blushing gums

clasped by roo paws
and silver dollars

bundled in brown paper
string bow

a eucalyptus euphemism for
'F#ck that sucks, Babe'

to accompany the
socks her folks got me —
shrimp pink flamingos

to dance me
with back-bending knees
into this
unknown.

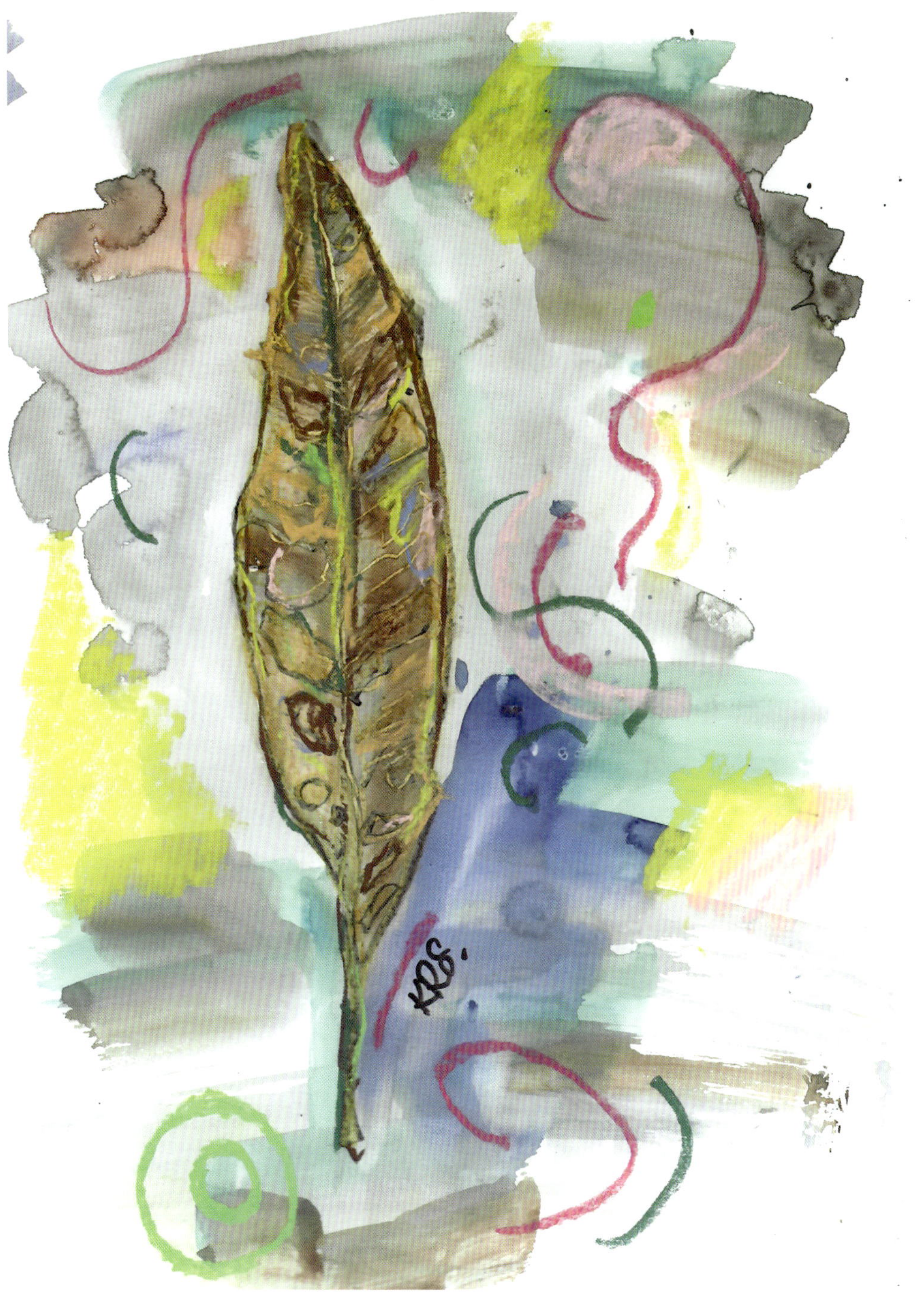
KRS.

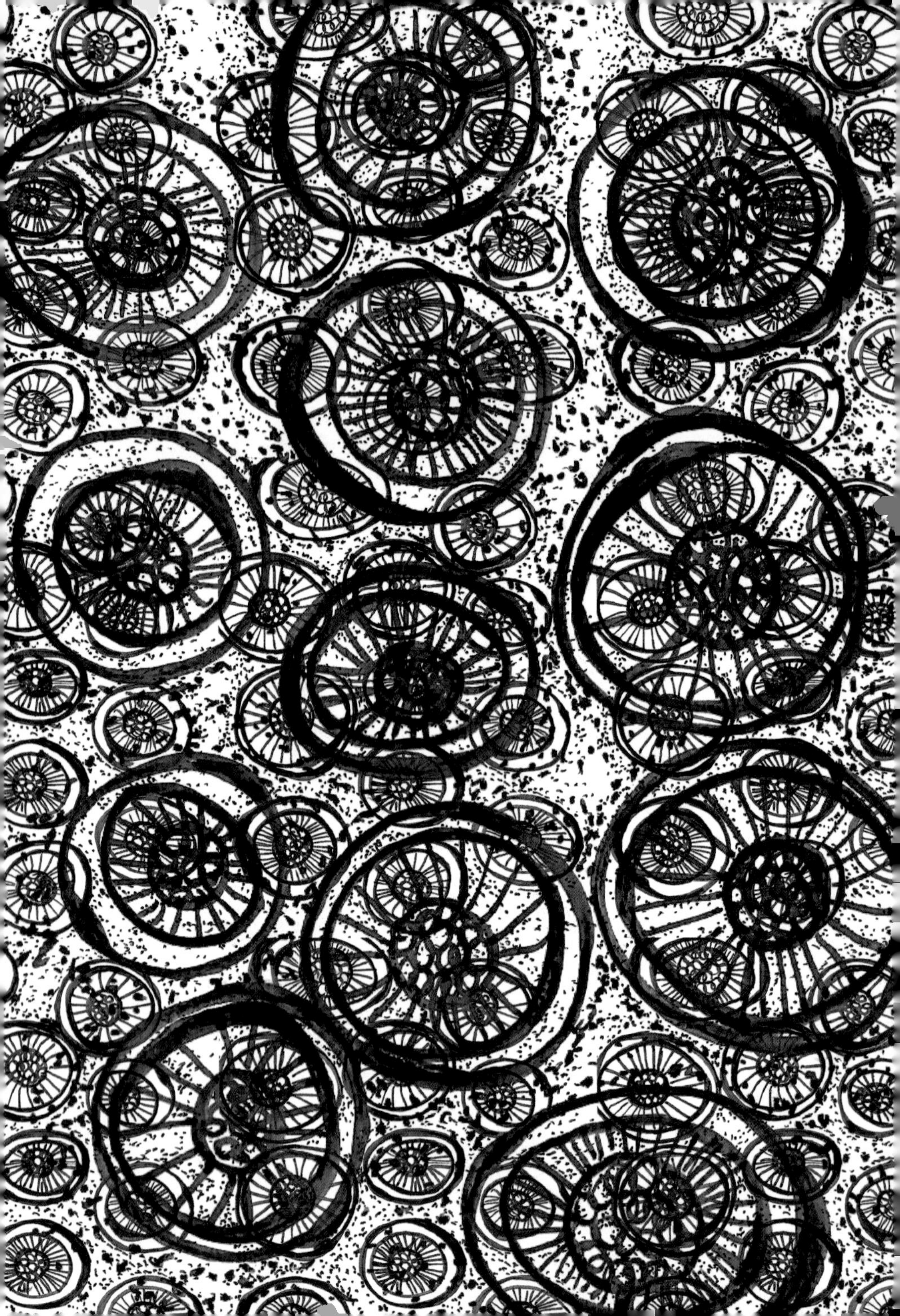

Appearances

~ After John O'Donohue

We have never seen our own faces
just reflections
in rear view mirrors
and shop fronts

have never known the love
in our eyes
just the returned gaze
of the objects
of our affections

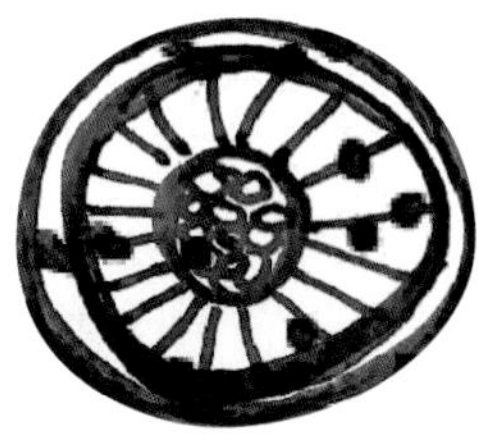

have never watched our lips
curl into smiles
our lips
smack and pout
and part —
just the fragments
of their actions
caught in selfies
and kisses

have never witnessed our cupids bow
bow to greet coffee
or fresh bread

our chins
pressed down to heart in namaste

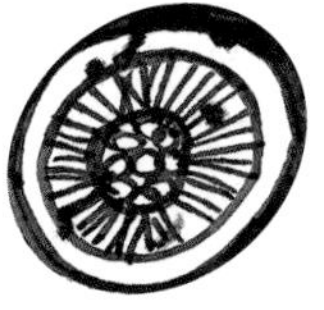

our cheeks
wet with tears
waking us from lucid dreams

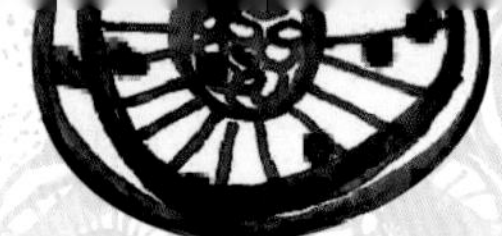

our brows
furrowed in thought

our freckles
like constellations

our complexions
mottled maps

we have never seen our own faces.

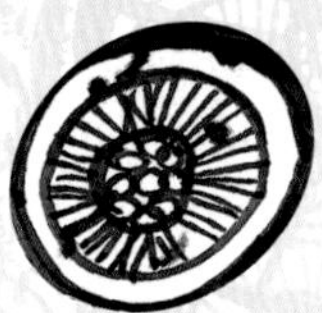

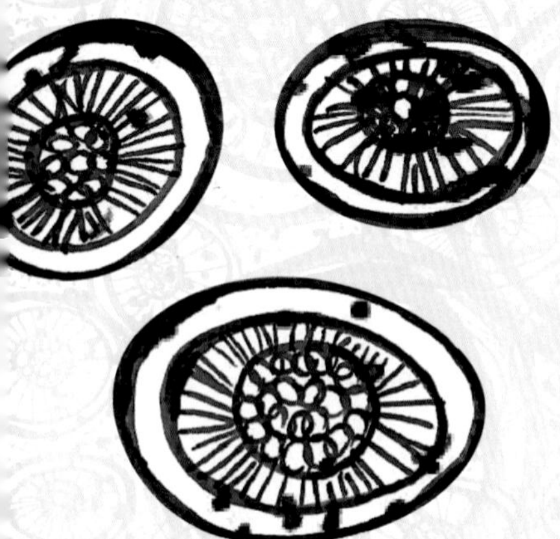

Messages from the Mat

~ With thanks to my yoga teachers and
my teachers' teachers

Life has its suffering

instability inevitable

so we tame turbulent senses
with discipline

subdue the spinning mind
that carries us away
from presence

move to cultivate stillness

press face against the glass
of anger
rage
frustration
and remain outside
the mind's protest.

We rest
in the challenge
and pain
where the teachings live
vast
and closest to source
permanent and peaceful
confidence and curiosity swelling.

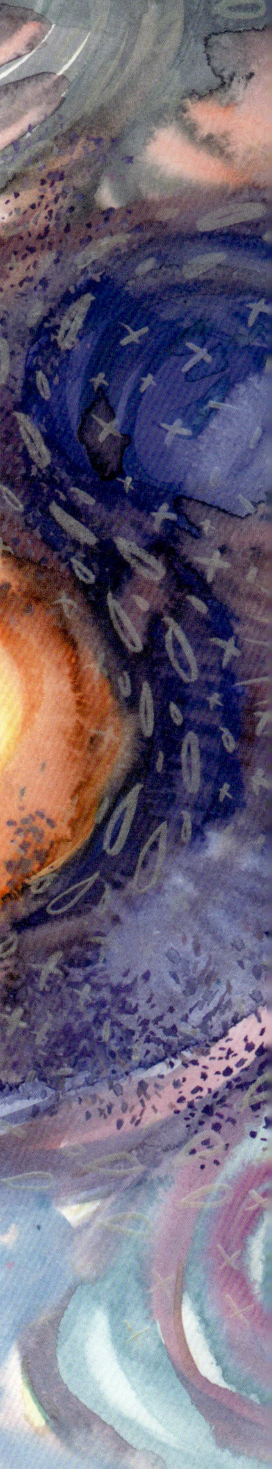

all issues are impermanent

and with consciousness continuous

nothing is too much to handle.

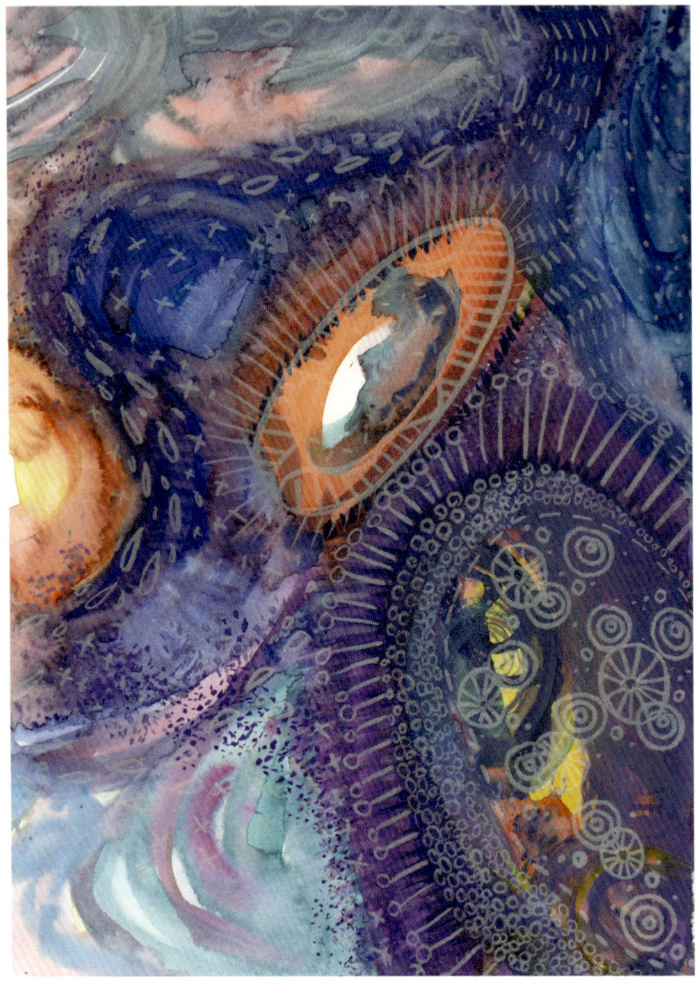

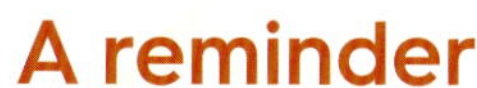

A reminder

~ For the survivors, with love

On the days
when your trauma parts
are louder than your grace

when your face contorts
with hate

and rage becomes you

when you've enacted every hack
but the pain still remains
and you reach for a vice —
anything to make life
just
bearable

I will stay by your side

someone to remind you
of the light
inside you —
always worthy of love
and belonging

and not for your productivity
or offerings to others
and the world

but for your darling
soul spark
aflame even in the darkest moments —

a potent wish of
Ancestors | God | The Universe

embodied like this for a lifetime

always one with The Divine

and inherently
always
enough.

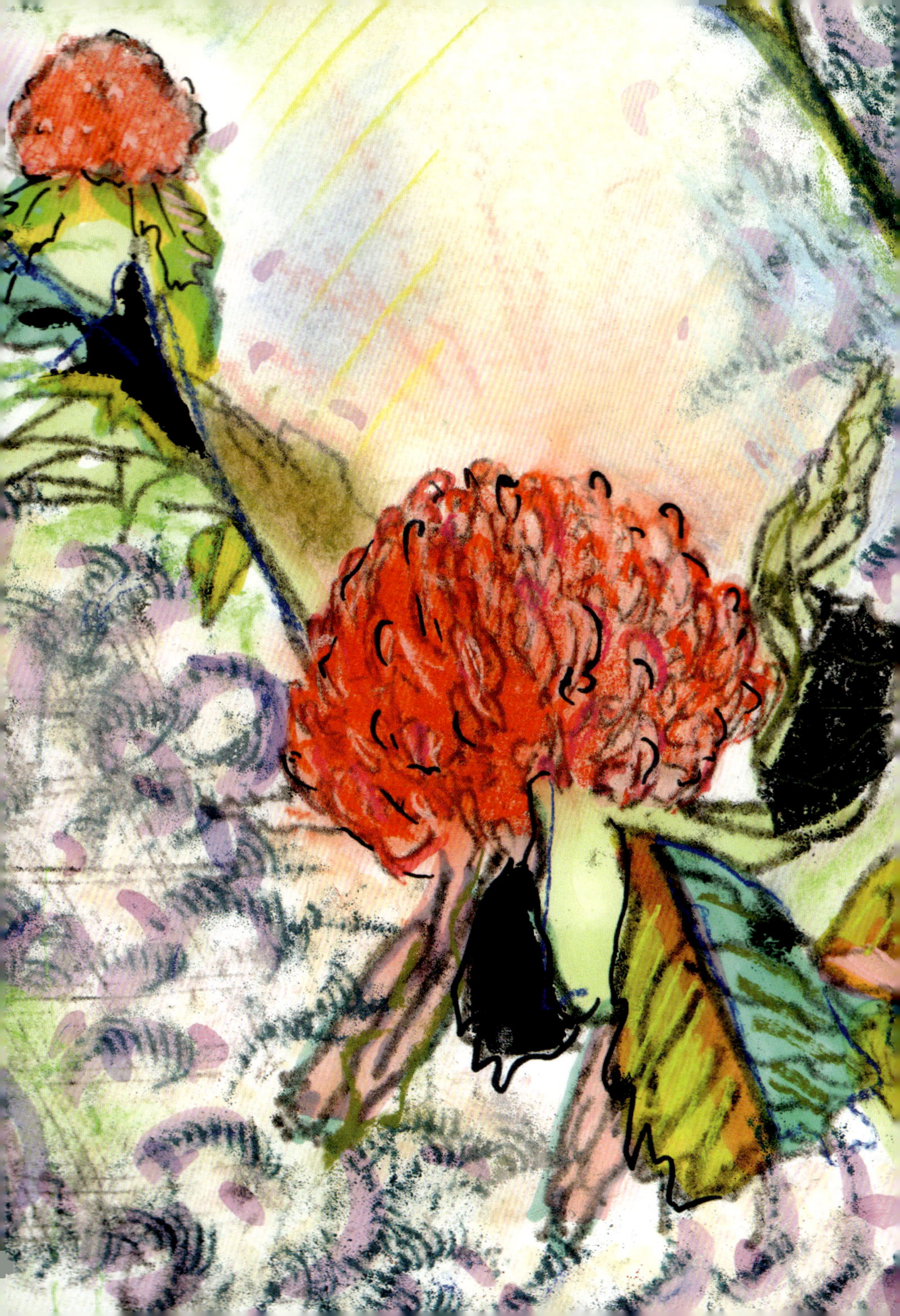

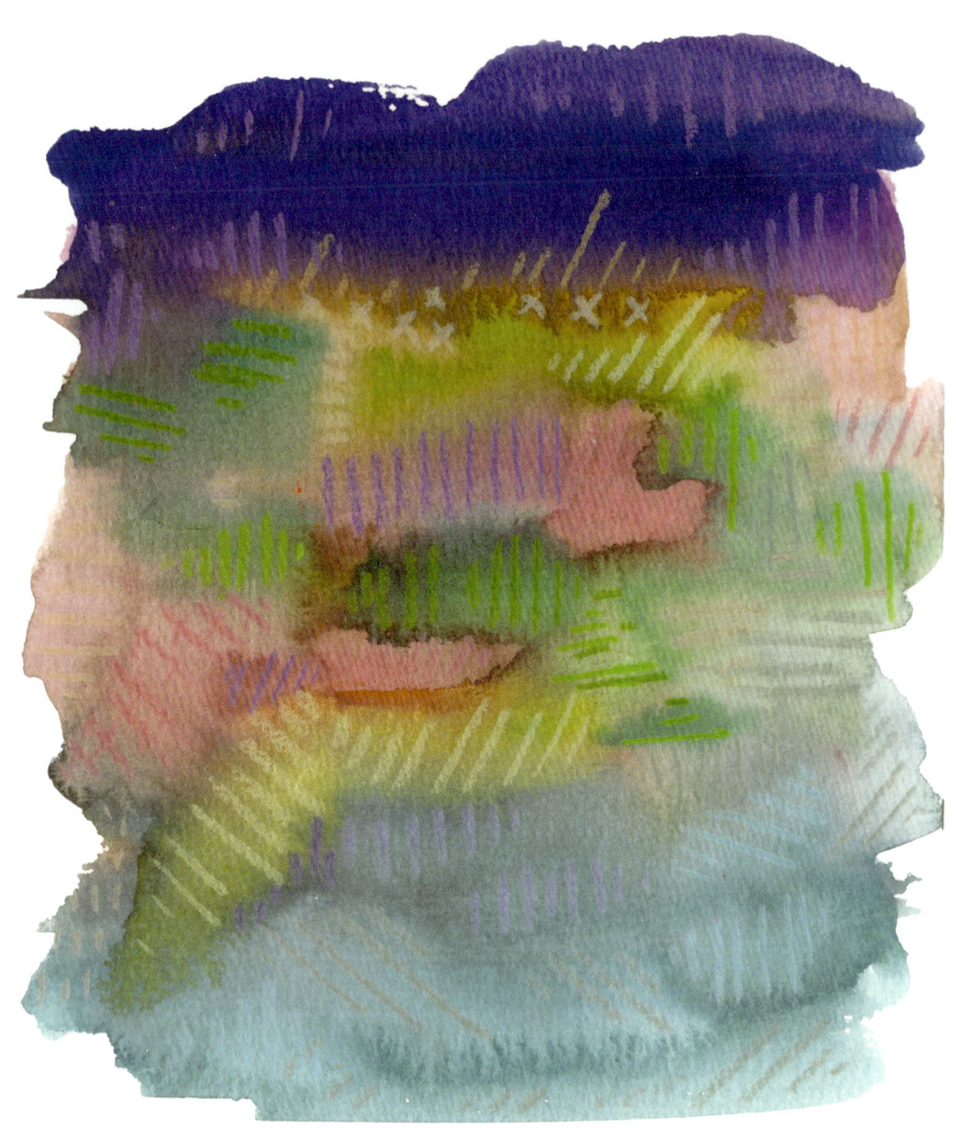

We see better with our Eyes Closed

~ With love for Marc and your yin calm and care

Have you ever
felt your way
through the darkness —
        fumbled
through the familiar
as if it were
        unknown?
Ever run hand along
        wall
                stair rail
                        sideboard
to read the blueprint
of a space
with your touch?

Ever reached for the light switch
        h e a r t r a c i n g
to find it had been replaced
        with nothingness
at least for a beat

and in that nothingness
did you find your breath
rattling in rib cage
        erratic
fear and doubt
        aloud?

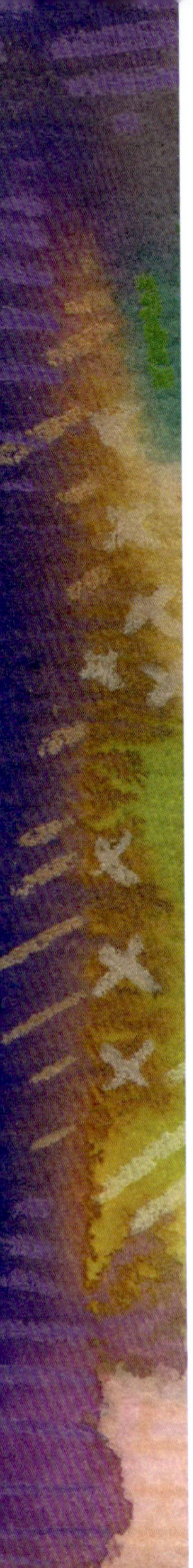

Did you still it
the way you know how?

eyes sealed —
        to better see

mantra —
        'this is temporary'

breath —
        wingspan wide and honeyslow

trust —
        in your teachings and the Old People.

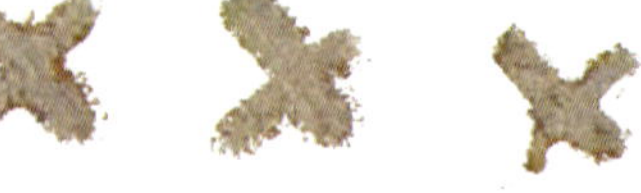

Butcher Bird Poem

~ With love and gratitude for Bec

I

In meditation
they teach us to find stillness —
union
with the body and breath

to realise that we are neither of these things.

As we release stories
open to pure
consciousness
calm and quiet
the segregation
dissipates

and we relate
with all

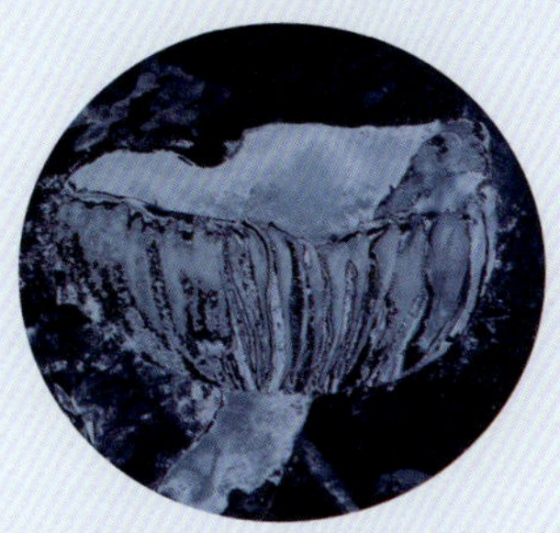

here we are nothing
and everything
at once

time and space
evaporate

and we are connected.

II

In the sun after class
I place golden kitchari in the palm
of my hand
turn it upwards
and revisit what we found

I settle in the sounds
of wind tousling trees
and a butcher bird
lands to eat

he eyes me warily
edges slowly
and as he feeds

unity finds shape.

In these silent moments
of sharing
I understand why we meditate —

not to separate
but to bind
to resonate
and to find

shared soul-sparks
with other spirits
in every form.

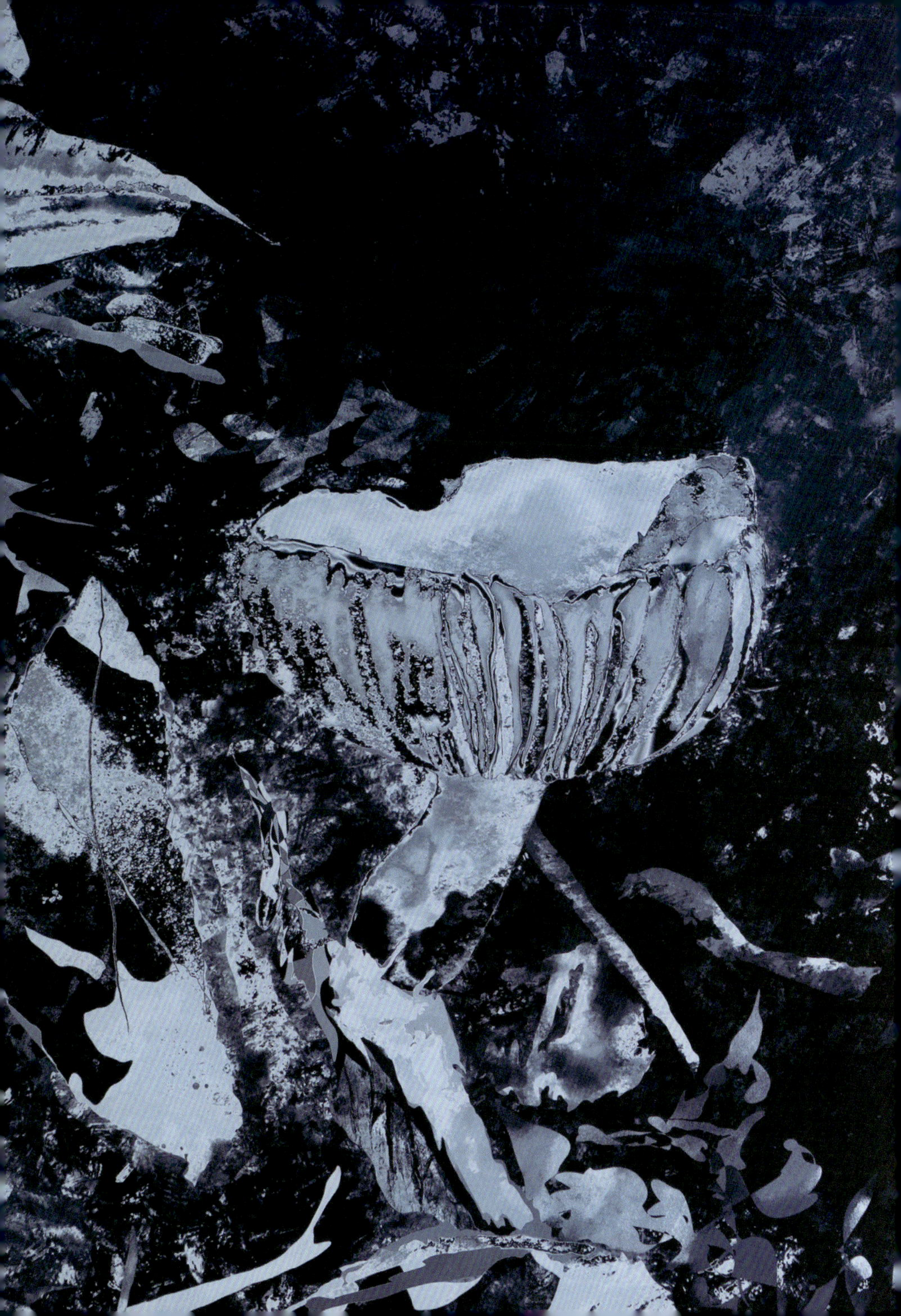

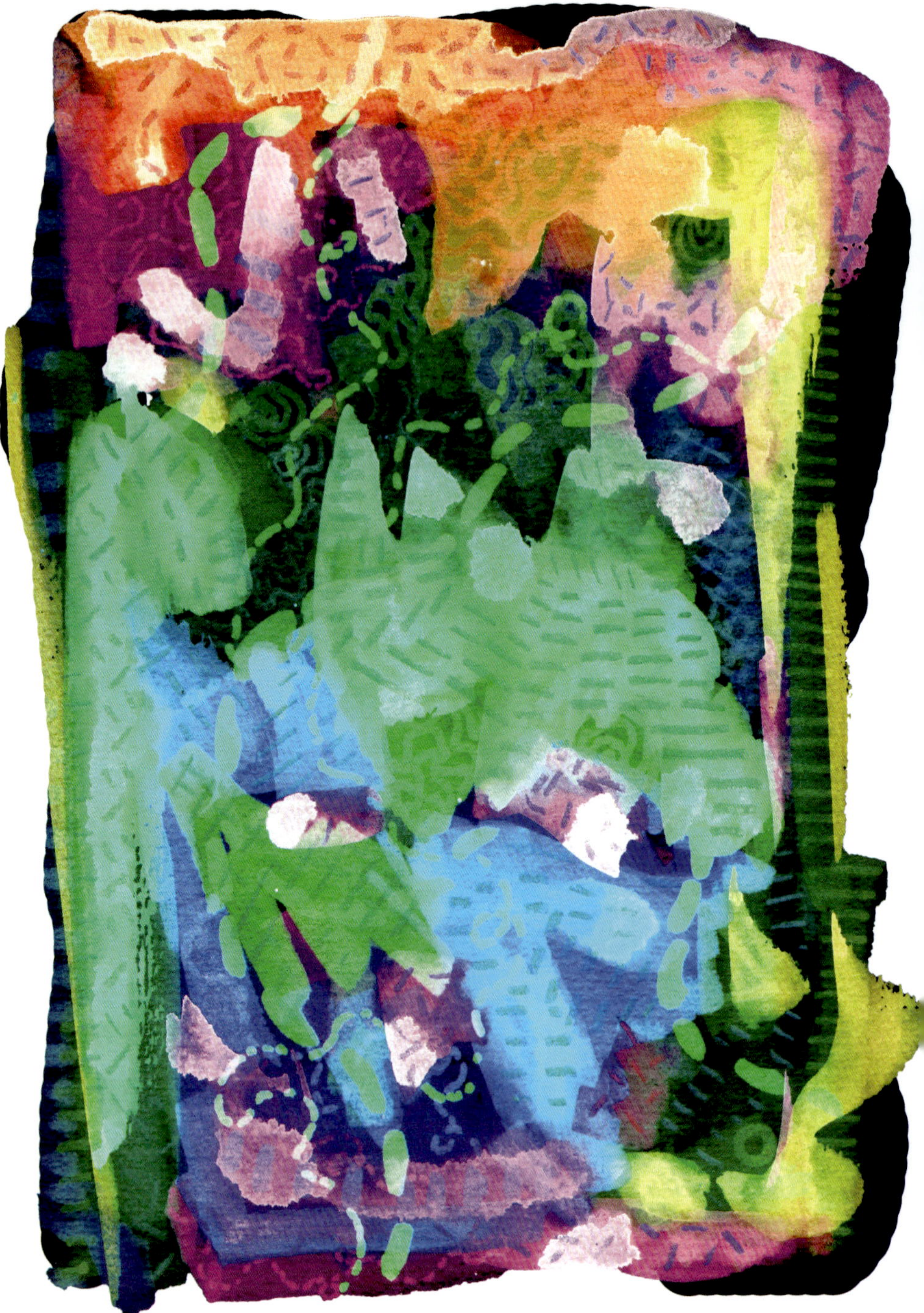

Healers

It is time to attend to the aches

to shake the memory
from fascia

to breathe
into the trauma torrents
scattered about your being

to speak strength
into scars
carved by generations of harm

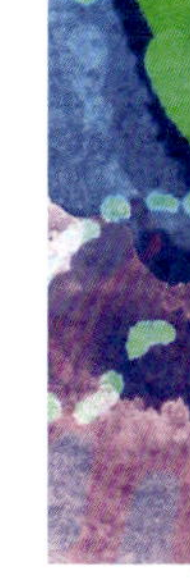

to regenerate Community | Family | Self
where otherness lays

to reclaim reign
over realm

to write affirmation
everywhere

so that deep Ancestral love
knows the way

love *always* knows the way.

Cleva

~ For my Brother boy, the Cleva one, with love

Brother boy tells me of the golden hour
talks me through what it means to collect firewood in the eve
to contemplate a day's happenings
to feed her flames
with any negative moments
to be freed
in the afterglow
of their release

to walk the cusp of sea and sand
at dawn
to be where
inky water mark-makes her way
to pervade busy-ness
before the day
on the yolk stained shore

he talks me through letting go —
unsubscribing from
preconceived limitations

says we need to forgo
the aspirations
fed to us by a dominant and deficit culture

to live more fully in alignment
with Mother Earth

to feel the worth she sees in us

to feel the rhythms of sea and sky and land

within and without

to stand with hand on heart
more often

entranced with
coming home

to who we truly are.

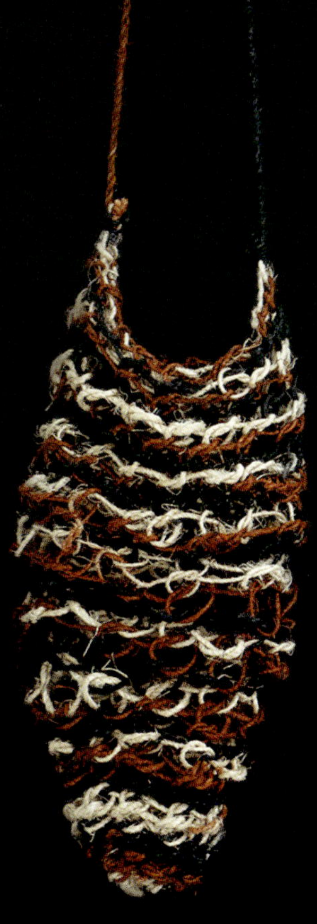

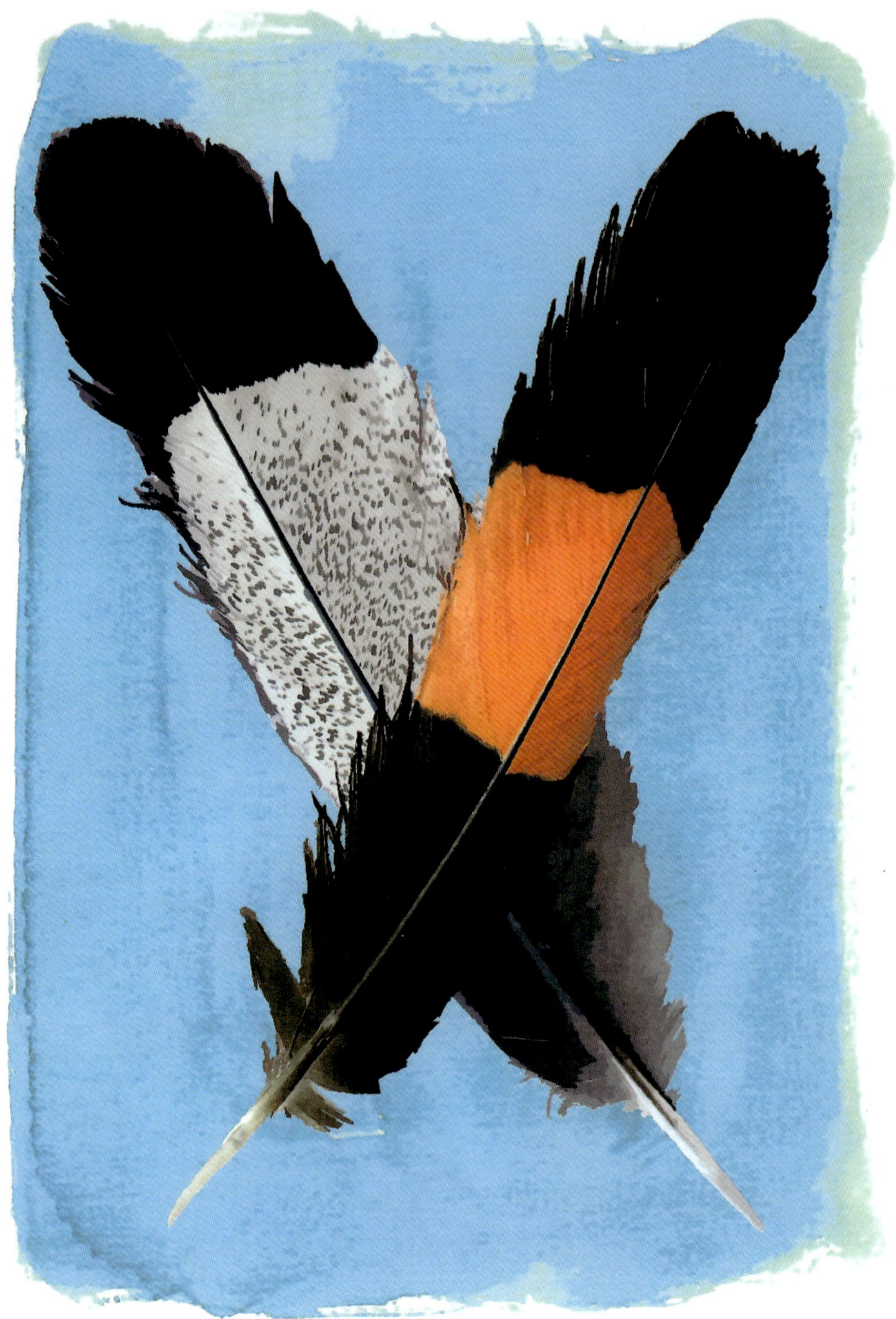

Adore – a found poem

~ After Adrienne Maree Brown, who taught me about desire and black joy

Black cockatoo chanting | black coffee in pannikin | pindan dust | fresh out of bed uttanasana | coals smouldering in sunshine, waiting for the next fire | Utthita Parsvakonasana | the first wave | the last | being called Aunty | calling her Aunty | Rooibos tea, almond milk and honey | my nephew's cheeky nose-scrunching smile | trying to hug Nan without triggering her fall-warning alarm | Mum's Banana cake — still warm | all the waratahs at Home | my brother's big belly laugh filling the room | lyrebirds chattering and on the move | echidna spine gifts | emu earrings made by sis | false sarsaparilla blooming bold | bush walks when it pours, the cabbage palm leaves loud | stringy bark rope twisted while yarning | Dad and his kookaburra feeding time | ant trains | Pop's hoya growing on the windowsill | My sister's going-home-now hug | fledgling birds and their swoopy Mums | all the plants I've ever given anyone | horse rides through the Kimberley | weaving from devil's twine and hemp | every feather | every smooth pebble | fingers gliding over fret | fresh black artliner pens | birthday swims with friends | covid dance-droughts being broken to a Jack River song | the first shower after camping in the desert | homemade mulberry pie | ochre in my hand | ochre on my face | the sun marks that snake around those shapes | smoking ceremonies that linger in your hair until the next day | being sung home by a lover | roo tails cooked old way, sucked off the bone | all the loves I've ever known | and outgrown | blunnies and jeans that fit just-right | bare feet on grass | the carry-on sand in my car seats and surf tub | the rings I've inherited | fresh sheets on a bed I didn't have to make | waking up in a swag | waking up to an unknown coast | Prasarita Padottanasana | lilly pilly pink | peppermint tea | pigface fruit popping sun on my tongue | leather jacket sliding cold over skin | the dry clutch rattle of a ducati | time and space to fill | time and space kept blank | expansive meditation | market meandering | a guitar being played by my love | poems sent to me | Elder trees | childhood photos with matchy matchy clothes | time with the fam | all of them at ease | the sea |

the wind howling up the casuarinas | the star imprint of their seed pod on thumb | a hockey ball hitting a backboard | the first mango of the season | the last one | cherry stains | songs played on repeat | books I reread | movies viewed from the bath | the books rehomed and those I kept | lockdown chats on the phone with friends | spray paint rattling cans | kelpie snugs | artists talking shop | trusted hugs from missed ones | yarning with mentors | Pop's paintings on my wall | voicemails from times before | water when I'm thirsty | learning the language of the land I'm on | whales breaching | plant dyeing with flowering gum | sewing my niece's quilt with Nan and Mum | rain on a tin roof | tulsi tea in op shop mugs | stars shooting in the Red Centre | noise-making for the joy of it | the quiet of a gallery | the stickiness of Dad's camp oven roast | gigs when the audience sings along real slow | summer lychees | the coolamons we cut from ancient bark | the art born on the balcony of a tiny home | dancing in mud at blues | accoustic claps ringing out | Tall Mountain ash on Gran's Country | Whip bird crests | bellbird song | bush orchids | waterholes | sarvasana | waking with Grandfather Sun |

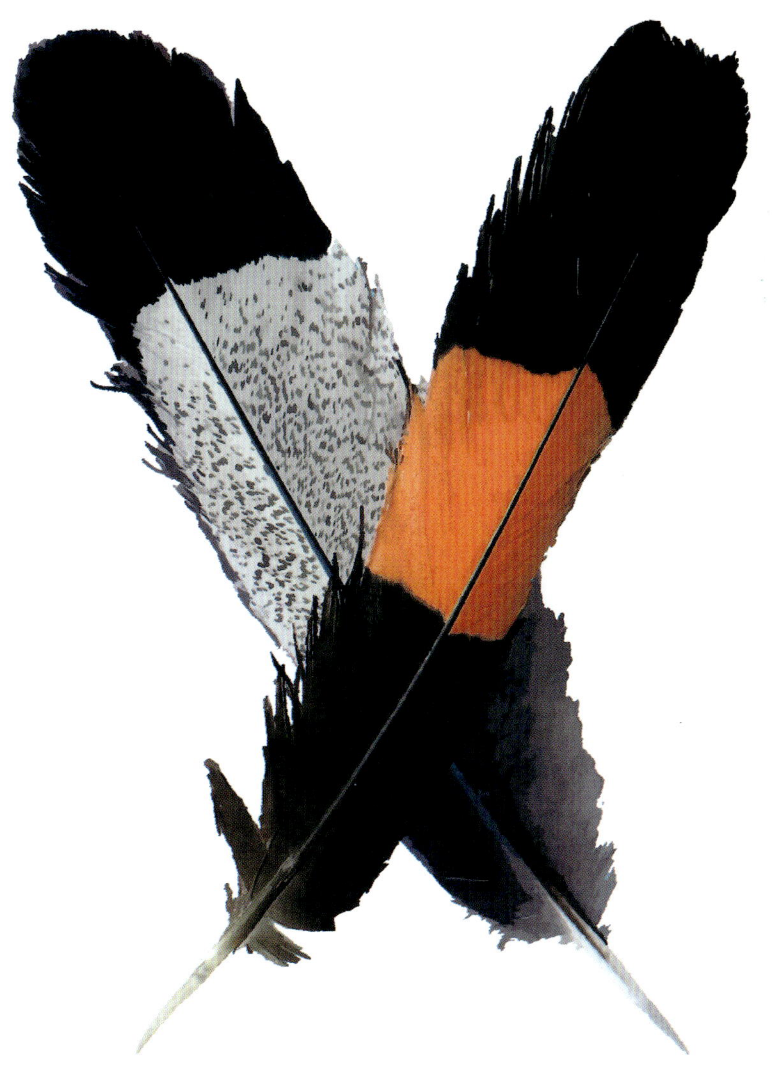

Sun Downs and Seasons

~ Written on Dharawal Country with deep respect to the Dharawal People who always have and will care for the land, seas and skies, and after Leanne Simpson, who offered the land as pedagogy, and helped me to dream and create realities in spite of settler occupation

this is the time
of lilly pillies
plumping into
(fullness)

Possum Skin Cloaks
on the mend
or perhaps being
worn for the first time
again

an age of deciduous
home makers
Losing
\lea|ves/

and the last
flowers
f
a
l
l
i
n
g
from myrtle

A moment
of wattle
and whale
syncing

to mark the start of
m i g ra t i o n

and like the Old Ones
here I am
healing
releasing
growing
and moving

fruiting a new path
on this Country
that is not mine

but who kindly
offers wisdoms
as trees

remind us
how our Scars
can be sacred

and the many ways
to lay down
deep
roots

to nourishment
beneath

even when the <<West Wind>>
howls and hauls

islands into o~c~e~a~n.

These wise ones
show how a crowded canopy
offers shade

but limits growth
of those below

knowing that
tall trees are
forged over
Grandfather
Sun Downs
and
seasons
seasons
seasons
seasons
seasons
seasons

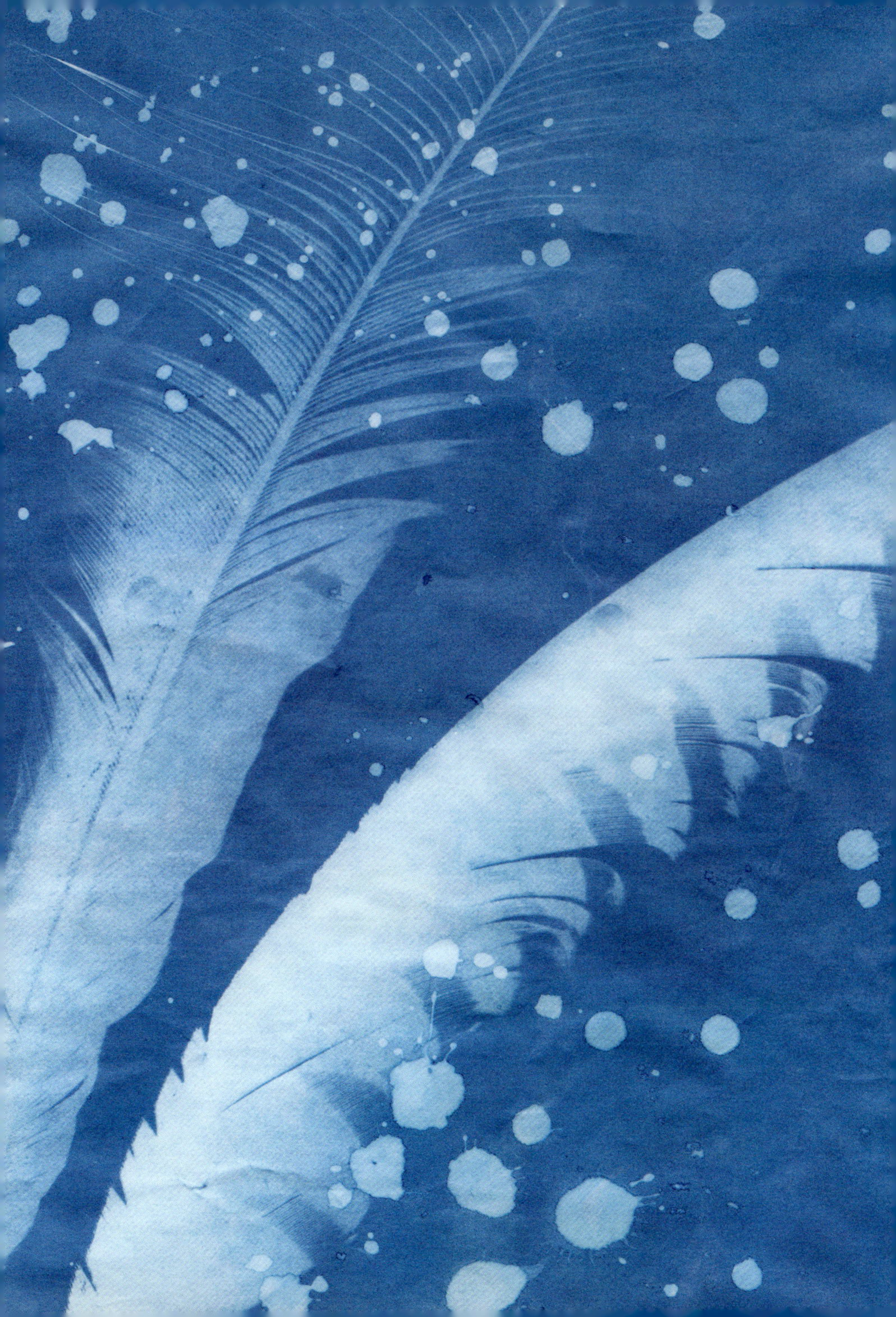

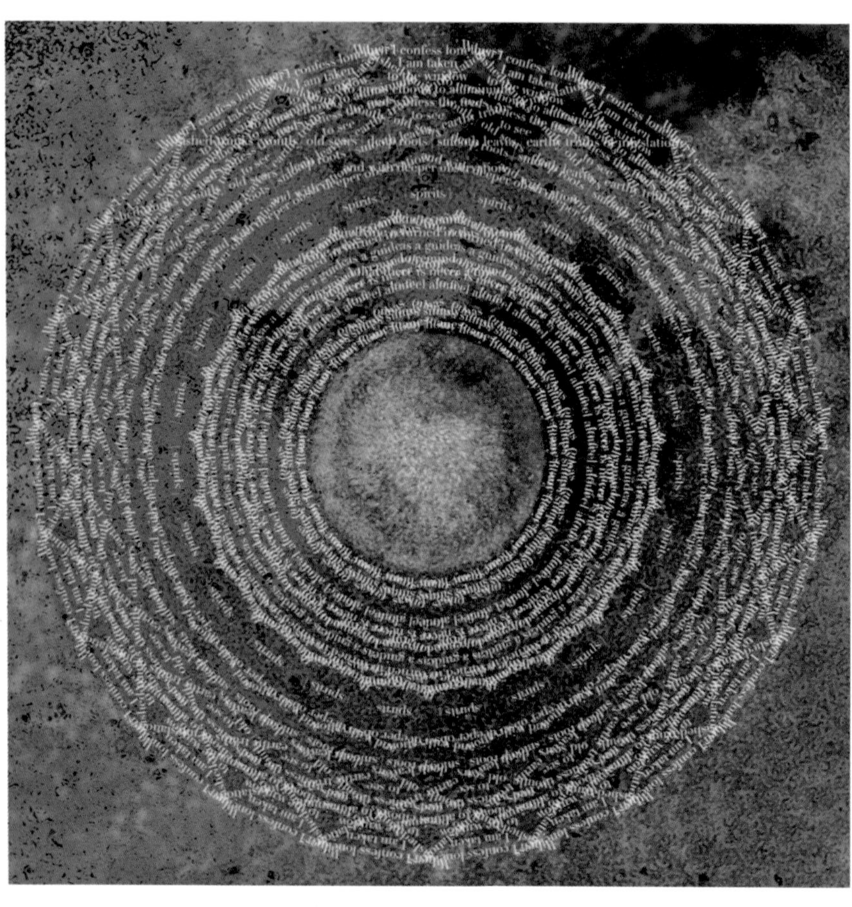

Oneness

~ For all the Blak poets, who understand the spirit in all things,
and appreciate the company of trees

When I confess loneliness
I am taken
to the window
to press elbows to aluminium
and witness the trees
to see

rashed trunks | youth | old scars | deep roots | smooth leaves | earthy truths
of infestation

and with deeper observation —

| spirits |

akin to mine
the divine returned in this lifetime
as a guide
to remind
that there is never a time
to feel alone —

oneness simply has
many homes.

CONTEXT

Returning was a poetic arts project which culminated in a visual poetry art exhibition, originally shown at SHAC Gallery, Gundungurra Land, in 2021. The 43 artworks shown in the exhibition were derived from the poems which were written for this collection.

This collection, *Returning,* spans themes of decolonisation, self-determination, truth-telling, the First Nations Matriarchy, queerness, justice, blak joy, love and liberation.

Returning is presented in four sections, Ochre + Eco glitter, Kin + Country, Rage + Grace, and Healing. Each poem has an accompanying visual poem; an artwork that was created to inspire the poem initially, or made in response to it.

The art for this project has been assisted by Oranges & Sardines Foundation, The Illawarra Women's Health Centre, Red Room Poetry, Magabala Books, Wollongong Art Gallery, Red Earth Arts Precinct, Bundanon Trust and predominantly by the Australian Government through the Australia Council for the Arts, its arts funding and advisory body.

It takes a community to raise a book baby, especially an experimental, blak and queer visual poetry collection. I was blessed with the best for this one, working again with the Dream Team at Magabala Books, and with industry leaders Rachel Bin Salleh and Grace Lucas-Pennington and Melena Cole-Manolis, Anna Moulton, Xenica Ayling, Gene Eaton and Kate Rendell.

This project in both its forms (the 2021 art exhibition and this collection) were created in collaboration, and with generous mentorship and guidance, from First Nations Elders, Custodians, consultants, artists, editors, academics and publishers to whom I am incredibly grateful. I would like to heartily acknowledge and offer my sea-deep thanks to Adrian Webster, Dr Lilly Brown, Genevieve Grieves, Aunty Loretta Parsley, Aunty Sharralyn (Shas) Robinson, Stephanie Beaupark, Grace Lucas-Pennington, Kylie Caldwell, David Cragg and Rachel Bin Salleh for their shaping of the poems and artworks that exist here.

For the ongoing lessons in Gundungurra Language, a language on Pop's side, and that of the land that raised us — thank you Aunty Velma Mulcahy and Aunty Sharyn Halls, and through her, the work of Jim Barrett. For the lessons in Dharawal, Gumea Dharawal and Dhurga — Mum and Nan's language, yadingji my brothers, Adrian Webster, Drew Longbottom, Jacob Morris, Joel Deaves and Ray Timbery.

For the photographs of the exhibition which live here now, thank you Sarah Tedder. For the photos of Mate You're Standing on Stolen Land, thank you Anna Warr and Wollongong Art Gallery. For the *Wallflowers and Evergreens* Film, thank you Tad Souden, and my family. For the filming, artistic mentorship, and exhibition assistance, thank you, Dr Tamryn Bennett, Jill Talbor, Robyn Kinsella, Brooke Munro, Karla Hayes, Clare Foale, Sarah Honey and Kaz Mcgrath.

And to my family, Mum, Dad, Nan, Jess, Zo, Sammy, Mila, Pip, Dunc, my loves, my friends, my housemates, my broader community and so many others who've been with me as I wrote this collection, and who supported my decision to freelance full-time and in a global pandemic. Who supported me when I came out. Who stood by my side at all the rallies. Who bushwalked, yarned, cried, swam, danced, wove, sewed and made coolamons with me, who drove me when I couldn't, who travelled with me, home and through the desert, mountain and rainforest, to river and the sea, and who assured me that my art, my words, my honesty was/is welcome —

Thank you.
I am nothing without you.

notes

Poems within *Returning* have also been supported by other publications and received recognition:

Aftermath First commissioned by Red Room Poetry.

Black Cars Winner, 2019 University of Canberra ATSI Poetry Prize.

Gugubara | Jerra | Guudhaa (Kookaburra | Star | Baby) Performed for Melbourne Writers Festival for Science Vs Romance with thanks to sis, Krystal De Napoli, 2020.

Kinship Country First appeared in *Cordite Poetry Review*, issue 104: KIN, 1 February 2022.

Oneness First published in *Going Down Swinging* #40, 2019.

Sacred Women Ways First published in *Borderless: A transnational anthology of feminist poetry*, Recent Work Press, 2021 with thanks to Aunty Yvette Holt.

Sun Downs and Seasons First commissioned by Red Room Poetry.

They Sung Us First appeared in *Cordite Poetry Review*, issue 106: OPEN, 15 September 2022.

~~title~~ | Tidal Shortlisted for Oodgeroo Noonuccal Indigenous Poetry Prize, 2021. Originally performed for Visions of Us at Sydney Opera House, with thanks to Jack River.

Vinegar and Bicarb First appeared in *Cordite Poetry* Review, issue 89: DOMESTIC, 1 February 2019.

Yabun (formerly titled Korrobori) Shortlisted for the Nakata Brophy Prize, 2020.

You can't pray the Gay out of me First appeared in *NANGAMAY dream MANA gather DJURALI grow*, BLACKBOOKS, 2023.

Several of the poems in *Returning* respond to the work of thought leaders, academics, artists, filmmakers, musicians and writers whose studies, essays, poems, podcasts and films have grounded and expanded my thoughts and process in recent years. A list can be found in the teacher's notes for *Returning* on the Magabala Books website.

Index of artwork

In order by appearance.

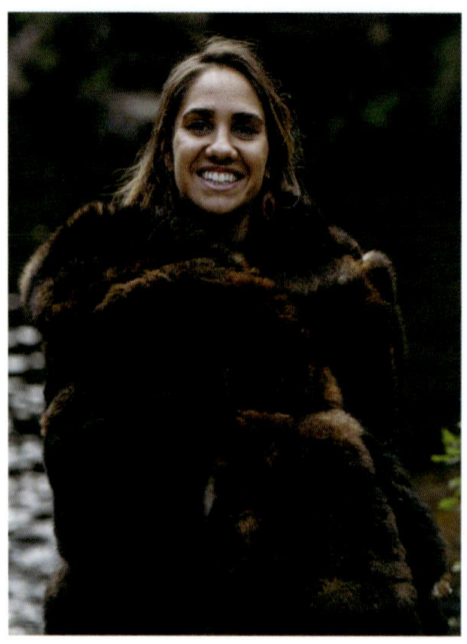

Kirli Saunders (OAM) is a proud Gunai woman and an award-winning author, multidisciplinary artist and consultant. An experienced speaker, facilitator and advocate for the environment and equality, Kirli was the NSW Aboriginal Woman of the Year (2020). In 2022, she was awarded an Order of Australia Medal for her contribution to the arts, particularly literature.

Kirli has partnered with global organisations including Google, Fender, Qantas, Spotify, Sydney Opera House, Mecca and Aesop to celebrate stories and cultivate change. Her celebrated books include *Bindi* (Magabala Books, 2020), *Our Dreaming* (Scholastic Australia, 2022), *Kindred* (Magabala Books, 2019), *The Incredible Freedom Machines* (Scholastic Australia, 2018) and the forthcoming *Returning* (Magabala Books, 2023). She is currently writing her anticipated novel, *Yaraman*, assisted by the Australia Council for the Arts.